THE COMPLETE
CRAZY
PATCHWORK

■ A N N E   H U L B E R T ■

■ FROM VICTORIAN BEGINNINGS
■ TO CONTEMPORARY DESIGN ■

B T Batsford • London

Dedicated to the little Hulberts:

Freya, Lucy, Ellie and Jemma

A special thank you to my editors, Jane Donovan and Diana Lodge, for their tremendous support and encouragement

First published 2002
© Anne Hulbert 2002

All illustrations except for the embroidery diagrams (see page 142)
by Anne and Denis Hulbert

All photography by Michael Wicks except for pages 17, 18, 19, 20, 54, 56, 66, 68 (top left), 71 and 81 by Ian Cole

ISBN 0 7134 8646 5

A CIP catalogue record for this book is available from the British Library.

Printed in Spain

for the publishers

B T Batsford
64 Brewery Road
London N7 9NT
England
www.batsford.com

A member of the Chrysalis Group plc

CONTENTS

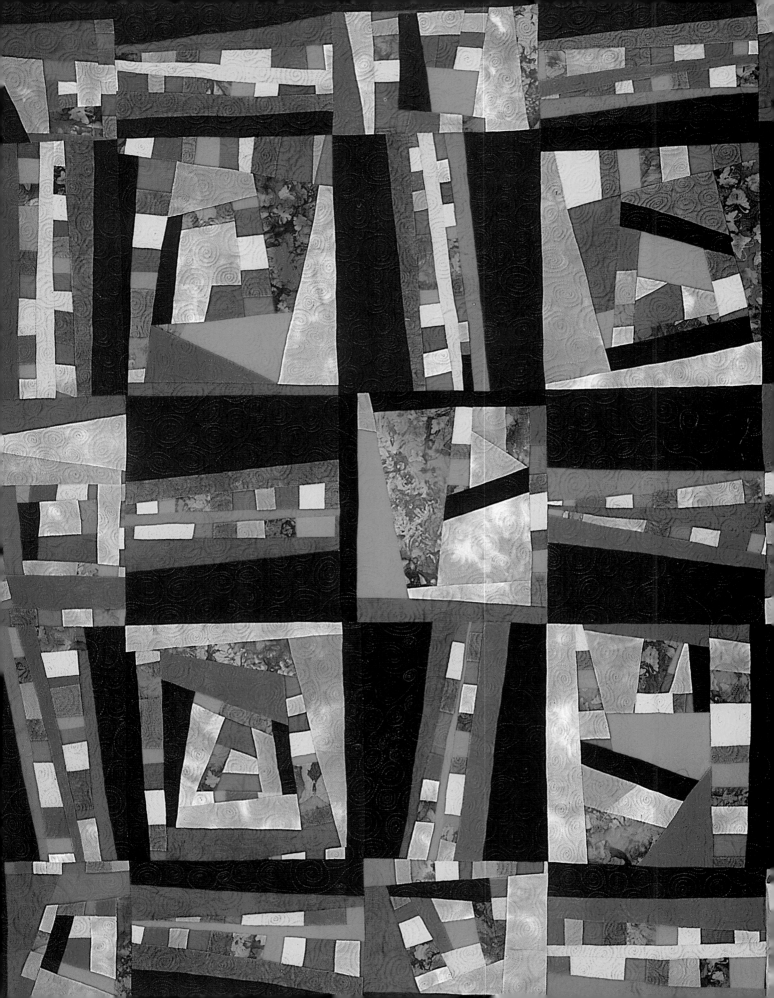

INTRODUCTION

***Patchwork without templates? ... Sounds crazy!
It is crazy - it's Crazy Patchwork!***

This book is a comprehensive guide to a most exciting form of patchwork – one that has not previously been fully explored. It investigates a wide range of techniques, from the heavily over-embellished Victorian, to the chic and minimalist styles of today. Some uncommon and interesting fabrics, as well as the more traditional types, are fully examined, as are the newer and rather unusual styles of ornamentation.

Crazy patchwork is an informal and versatile form of needlework, with little or no set design. Almost any fabric can be used. The work is very individual and allows tremendous freedom of expression. It has exuberance and is unique in its eccentricity of colour, arrangement and decoration. It is never boring. While Victorian crazy patchwork was generally managed without templates, I have provided patterns for one or two of the projects. Their purpose is to encourage the beginner to become involved in this lovely, uninhibited form of patchwork. The book includes several projects for the reader who wishes to experiment with this type of work. These incorporate a range of techniques, such as Victorian style crazy patchwork, crazy log cabin and crazy strip patchwork. There are fashion items and accessories, articles for the home and more.

For further inspiration, explore chapter 15 at the end of the book. This contains photographs of a spectacular collection of crazy patchwork – contemporary interpretations of quilts, hangings and smaller pieces – inspired by Victorian needlewomen.

Anne Hulbert – Berwick-upon-Tweed, September 2001

Frontispiece: This award-winning patchwork, machine pieced in a freeform style (contemporary crazy), was inspired by a workshop with Judith Trager. Measuring 94 x 104cm (37 x 41in), the patchwork is mostly of hand-dyed cottons. The work is machine-quilted. (Casa Loco by Janice Gunner)

Chapter One

THE HISTORY OF CRAZY PATCHWORK

Pre-Victorian crazy patchwork was to a large extent the product of poverty-inspired thrift. Many different kinds of fabric – flannel, cotton, woollen and linen – would be combined in one piece, regardless of shape, texture or colour. Nothing was wasted, every scrap and remnant being recycled to provide warm garments and bedding, with the patches cut out at random to replace oddly shaped worn areas. Similarly, good parts were saved from worn clothing and stitched to some stout fabric, such as a washed flour bag, which served as a foundation to bear the strain of wear and tear, as well as to provide warmth and comfort. Unfortunately, but perhaps not surprisingly, little of the earlier work has survived.

Nonetheless, some examples of this early utilitarian work must surely have filtered into the late 19th-century home, thus providing inspiration for diligent Victorian women. Here was an exciting new form of needlework to be explored, and at a time when a lady's fine clothes were a measure of her gentility. Scraps of precious silks, rich brocades and plush velvets, together with ribbons and laces,

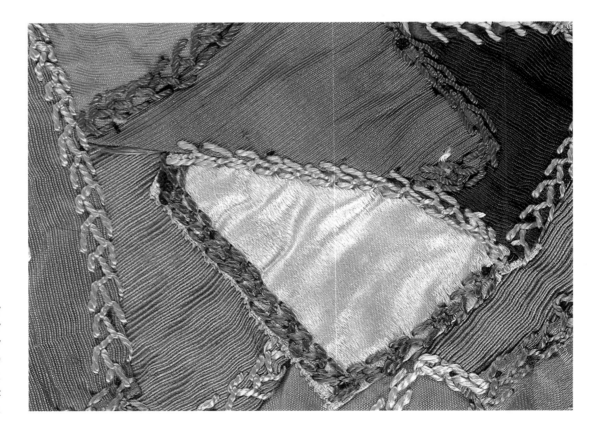

A tiny fragment of early 20th-century crazy patchwork, using a variety of fine silks. It is worked in feather stitch throughout, using many different colours of perlé threads.

were recycled from cast-off garments, including the ladies' full and cumbersome dresses and ball gowns, children's clothes, and maybe a wedding dress. Lush furnishings in opulent colours were also reclaimed. In this way, innumerable quilts, throws, table runners, cushions (pillows), tea cosies and many other accessories for the parlour and the boudoir were conceived.

After the patches had been basted to a foundation, the seams were elaborately embroidered with a gaudy variety of threads and stitches. Then came the real embellishments – buttons and bows, appliqué items, silk flowers, ribbons, lace, beads and feathers. Any available memento was given space so that the work became, in effect, a touchingly sentimental scrapbook or a record of events – a delightful *aide memoire*, decorated with a myriad of memorabilia.

Just as in a scrapbook, important events were recorded, with embroidered names and dates and a fragment of a wedding dress, a Valentine, scraps from a christening robe, or other novelty. Such memory-laden pieces speak volumes.

Good examples of Victorian crazy patchwork are certainly hard to find. Quilts, throws, cushions (pillows), mantelpiece fronts and novel pieces were made to be used, and well used they were. Those that have stood the test of time can be seen in the textile departments of British and American museums. Quilting and embroidery guilds also own some very fine and well cared-for examples that may be viewed.

The asymmetrical compositions that are so characteristic of Japanese design are thought to have influenced the late Victorian development of crazy patchwork, which may even have had its

Measuring 53 x 33cm (21 x 13in), this sofa throw dates from around 1890. Made from a wide variety of silks, brocades, satins, velvets and ribbons, it is a truly crazy piece, with its jumbled arrangement of unusual random-cut shapes. Many colours of a perlé-type thread were used for the ubiquitous feather stitching. The throw is trimmed with a border of handmade lace, 8cm (3¹/₄in) deep.

(From the author's collection)

An ornately decorated crazy patchwork quilt, circa 1887, is embellished with stars, a butterfly and a fan. The nine central blocks are surrounded by a wide border of blocks, and the quilt is lavishly embroidered and adorned with sequins, buttons and gold braid. An image of Queen Victoria's head and the date of her Golden Jubilee, 1887, are included. The quilt measures 163cm (64in) square. (From the Heritage Collection of the Quilters' Guild of the British Isles)

Opposite: The haphazardly arranged patches of this very fine late 19th-century crazy patchwork tea cosy are richly embroidered with a lovely array of floral designs. Every silk and velvet patch is decorated in glorious colours, and the quality of the embroidery is very high. Almost all the traditional stitches have been worked in plain and variegated threads. (From the Heritage Collection of the Quilters' Guild of the British Isles)

origins in the Orient. At the 1876 Centennial Exposition in Philadelphia the Japanese stand was regarded as very impressive, and drew crowds. Needlewomen of the day could relate the lines of the 'crazed and crackled' finish found on the oriental ceramics and textiles to the outlines of oddly cut crazy patches. An abundance of Japanese imagery, embroidery patterns, silk motifs and newly arrived novelties were soon to enhance their needlework.

Another possible influence was provided by the Chinese who, from the Sung Dynasty (960–1280) onwards, induced a network of very thin cracks on the surface of fine porcelain. This type of ware was fashionable in the Victorian home. Alternatively, the concept of crazy patches may have been inspired by craquelure – the network of fine cracks that often covered the surface of old paintings or their varnish.

Below: A cushion (pillow) front, from the early 1900s, measuring 53cm (21in) square. It is made from cottons, plain and printed velvets and needlecords. The seams are featherstitched throughout with six strands of yellow cotton. (From the author's collection)

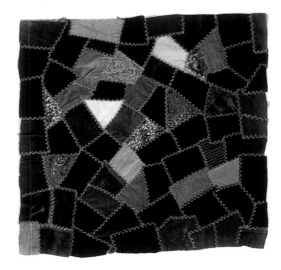

Whatever its origins, the vogue for crazy patchwork did not reach its zenith until around the 1880s, when this fashionable new form of needlework began to sweep America, England and Australia. *Godey's Lady's Book*, which was founded in 1838 and was one of the first women's magazines to be published in America, ran advertisements for 'Crazy Patchwork Kits' around 1885.

The exhaustive decoration and ornamentation that has already been mentioned became the watchword. With a typical Victorian obsession for over-statement, crazy patchwork quickly came to be smothered in an encrustation of beads, sequins, buttons, shells, ribbon work, quilting and appliqué. The incorporation of painted birds and flowers, photographs, cigarette silks and

A second cushion (pillow) front, dating from between 1898 and 1900, is made from fine silks and velvets, with seams worked over in yellow in very large feather and blanket stitches. The front measures 46cm (18in) square. *(Lent by Sarah Mitchell)*

Below: This violin cover, circa 1900, is an unusual example of crazy patchwork. Measuring 61cm (24in) long and from 10 to 23cm (4 to 9in) wide, it was designed to be laid over the violin when in its case. The cover is made from beautiful silk satins, brocades and decorative wide silk ribbons. The bold and heavy embroidery is splendid: bands of pattern are worked on the ribbon stripes, elements of the fabric designs are picked out, and all-over stitching is worked on the smaller prints. Fairly coarse threads in many colours are used. While there is a thick layer of cotton batting between the patchwork and the lining, the cover is not actually quilted.
(From the author's collection)

A detail of a quilt made in 1887 shows the ingenious arrangements of truly crazy patches, the variety of fine embroidery patterns, beadwork, the appliqué butterfly, couched with gold braid, and one of the eight-petalled flowers.
(From the Heritage Collection of the Quilters' Guild of the British Isles)

The crazy work of this sachet, measuring 23cm (9in) square, is made from a selection of fine late Victorian silks and brocades. The edges of the patches are turned under and worked entirely in feather stitch, using a variety of threads and colours. It is likely that the patchwork was first made for a cushion (pillow) front, and subsequently made into a sachet and bound with ribbon in the 1930s. (Lent by Sylvia Armstrong M.B.E.)

Far right: This well-used tea cosy from the early 1900s clearly saw service. While not as elaborately decorated as some, it has been painstakingly made from fine quality silks and brocades. Small closely worked feather stitching, in many colours, decorates the seams. Measuring 41 x 28cm (16 x 11in), it is trimmed with silk cord. (Lent by Sylvia Armstrong M.B.E.)

woven Valentine messages followed. While since considered by purists to be vulgar, ostentatious and inelegant, the colourful kaleidoscopic effect of such generous and lively embellishment is recognized as the distinctive hallmark of late Victorian crazy patchwork.

In the 1920s and early 1930s, crazy patchwork lost much of its former lavish style and decoration. Fabrics became less rich, and designs less inspired. The 1950s and 1960s saw signs of a return to crazy patchwork, perhaps influenced by the urban fashion for crazy paving, but with an attractive simplicity. Fewer adornments were added, and more use was made of the sewing machine. By then, this could offer fancy stitches, many being very passable imitations of hand stitches. Some crazy patchwork was quilted in classic patterns, but much was not quilted at all.

Since then crazy patchwork has made noticeable advances. It is now enjoying a welcome

revival, with fresh and innovative ideas and an inspired use of the superb contemporary fabrics, colours and textures. The work photographed in the Gallery at the end of the book reflects the freedom and individuality of crazy patchwork in contemporary design.

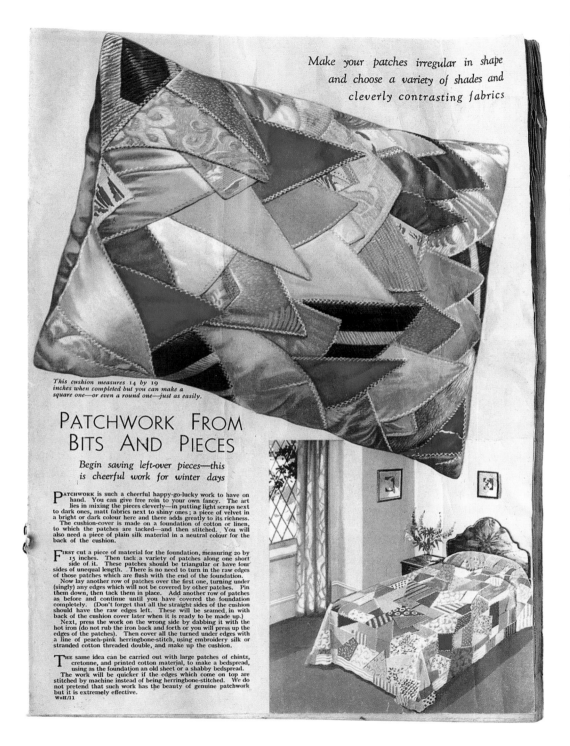

*Make your patches irregular in shape
and choose a variety of shades and
cleverly contrasting fabrics*

*This cushion measures 14 by 19
inches when completed but you can make a
square one—or even a round one—just as easily.*

PATCHWORK FROM BITS AND PIECES

*Begin saving left-over pieces—this
is cheerful work for winter days*

PATCHWORK is such a cheerful happy-go-lucky work to have on hand. You can give free rein to your own fancy. The art lies in mixing the pieces cleverly—in putting light scraps next to dark ones, matt fabrics next to shiny ones; a piece of velvet in a bright or dark colour here and there adds greatly to its richness.

The cushion-cover is made on a foundation of cotton or linen, to which the patches are tacked—and then stitched. You will also need a piece of plain silk material in a neutral colour for the back of the cushion.

FIRST cut a piece of material for the foundation, measuring 20 by 15 inches. Then tack a variety of patches along one short side of it. These patches should be triangular or have four sides of unequal length. There is no need to turn in the raw edges of those patches which are flush with the end of the foundation.

Now lay another row of patches over the first one, turning under (singly) any edges which will not be covered by other patches. Pin them down, then tack them in place. Add another row of patches as before and continue until you have covered the foundation completely. (Don't forget that all the straight sides of the cushion should have the raw edges left. These will be seamed in with back of the cushion cover later when it is ready to be made up.)

Next, press the work on the wrong side by dabbing it with the hot iron (do not rub the iron back and forth or you will press up the edges of the patches). Then cover all the turned under edges with a line of peach-pink herringbone-stitch, using embroidery silk or stranded cotton threaded double, and make up the cushion.

THE same idea can be carried out with large patches of chintz, cretonne, and printed cotton material, to make a bedspread, using as the foundation an old sheet or a shabby bedspread. The work will be quicker if the edges which come on top are stitched by machine instead of being herringbone-stitched. We do not pretend that such work has the beauty of genuine patchwork but it is extremely effective.

WoH/11

*In this patchwork feature
from a mid-1950s issue of
Woman and Home, the term
'crazy' is not mentioned.
The overlapping patches are
stitched to a foundation, with
the raw edges turned under.
Herringbone stitch in peach-
coloured embroidery silk is
worked over all the seams.*
(Lent by Sylvia Armstrong M.B.E.)

ChapterTwo

FOUNDATIONS, FABRICS & EQUIPMENT

One of the great advantages of crazy patchwork is that it can combine an infinite variety of both natural and synthetic fabrics. Depending on the function of the project, virtually anything can be used. There is an almost inexhaustible choice of dress and furnishing fabrics, including velvet, leather, metallic, glitzy and many other types of fabric with interesting textures, surface finishes and colours.

Crazy patchwork is addictive and, for that reason, at the first inclination to explore its potential you should start the hunt for fabric pieces. Buy because you like what you see – and buy a fabric when you see it, for it could be gone by tomorrow. The ideal piece of fabric can be very inspiring. Assemble a wide range of patterned, plain, striped and checked fabrics, collecting those with interesting textures, and building up a range from the lightest to the heavier weights. Experiment with brilliant and outrageous fabrics, and do not disregard tiny scraps, especially samples of luxury fabrics such as silks and metallics. Not only are these essential for filling awkward gaps, but it is often the tiniest scrap that is the most effective.

The selection of a fabric for a project requires careful thought. Is it appropriate for the purpose? Are its type, weight and texture suitable? Will it wear well, and can it be washed and ironed without dire results? Some fabrics should only be dry-cleaned, and it is as well to check this at the outset. When buying new fabrics, salespersons are usually pleased to advise, and many fabrics now carry details of their precise content, together with washing instructions.

A variety of richly textured fabrics for crazy patchwork.

FOUNDATION FABRICS

Crazy patchwork starts with a firm, non-stretch foundation that acts as a base on which to stitch the patches. The foundation should always be sufficiently stable to hold the weight of the patchwork, as well as any proposed decorations. While calico and other cottons make good foundations, discarded plain or printed fabrics can be used for the same purpose. Either side of the foundation can be utilized, as it will be covered, and using up oddments is more economical. The piece should be large enough for the project, however, as a whole-piece foundation will avoid the joins and seams that can weaken an otherwise stable fabric. Also, a seam can leave a ridge that will show on the front.

The selection of a foundation fabric must also have regard to subsequent hand embroidery. This is particularly important if you are joining the patches together at the same time as they are stitched to the foundation. It should be possible for a sewing needle, threaded with the selected thread, to pass through all layers of the foundation and patches easily without too much tugging and pulling. Struggling with the needle and thread can be painful and is liable to weaken and untwist the thread.

If you are using a sewing machine to join the patches, first try out the stitching on a prepared practice piece of the selected fabrics. A larger or smaller needle may be more satisfactory, or perhaps the needle or bobbin tension may require adjustment.

PATCHWORK FABRICS

Cotton Natural cotton weaves include broadcloth, calico, chintz, corduroy, cotton, denim, gauze, muslin (cheesecloth), poplin, sateen, twill and velveteen. Pure cottons are a good-tempered and comfortable group of fabrics to work with. When really necessary, they can be unpicked without ill effect. While some cotton fabrics may shrink and fade, there will be few problems with washing and ironing. Cotton fibres dye well, particularly with vegetable dyes, and are generally warmer to wear than synthetics.

Leather Many beautiful soft leathers, suedes and gloving kids are now available. These are often dyed in glorious colours or printed with lovely patterns, and there are also leathers with metallic surfaces, including gold, silver and bronze. These soft leathers

A collection of hand and commercially-dyed cotton fabrics, including different weights of furnishing, dressmaking weight, Japanese prints and American patchwork plains and prints.

Machine zigzag stitching was used to join the metallic leather crazy patches after these had been bonded to Filmoplast (fusible webbing suitable for leather). The design for covering a wastepaper bin (garbage basket) shows random-cut strips of leather and suede, also bonded to Filmoplast prior to machine stitching. Also shown are small samples of coloured patterned leather. (Spectacle case, measuring 15 x 9cm (6 x 3¹/₂in), by Rona Tarry; wastepaper bin design by Anne Hulbert)

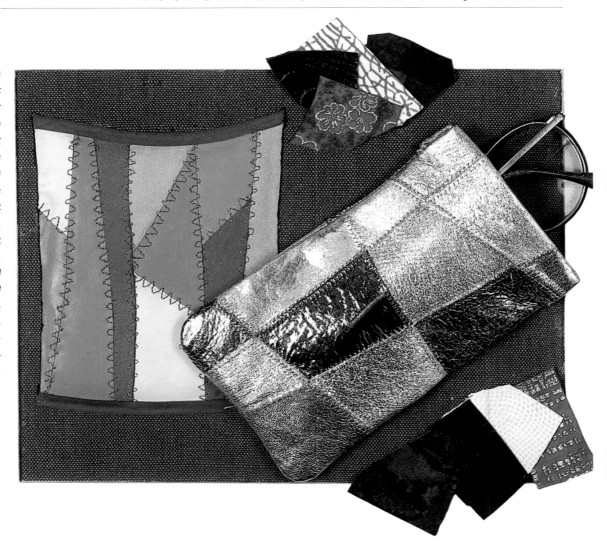

are very pliable and easy to machine stitch, and the resulting crazy patchwork fabrics can be used to produce very elegant bags, purses and a variety of fashion accessories. Soft leather pieces can also make very attractive motifs for appliqué.

Certain leathers can be ironed. Use a low heat, spread a dry cloth over the wrong side, and carefully iron lightly and smoothly over the surface. When joining leather patches, they must abut. Do not overlap the edges, as double layers leave unsightly ridges. There is also a self-adhesive material that is excellent for joining leather patches. Paper gum-strip will hold the edges together during the stitching, but it has a tendency to tear.

For stitching, use purpose-made leather needles, and either a Teflon-based foot, or a roller foot to help the leather through smoothly. Keep to a medium-to-large stitch to avoid making too many perforations and thus weakening the seam.

Linen Linen is a product of the flax plant. Linens range from very fine and lovely fashion fabrics to a heavier furnishing weight. A linen fabric will often be recognizable by its sheen and attractive slub texture. Linen dyes and washes well and can be ironed with a very hot iron. It does, however, have a tendency to fray, and its edges require protection against unravelling,

Metallics Metallic fabrics will always add a touch of luxury to patchwork, no matter how small the patch may be. A brilliant array is obtainable, gold, silver and bronze vying with reds, blues, pinks and greens. The only disadvantage to metallics is their tendency to fray, but this can be mitigated by backing them with an iron-on fusible interfacing. Use a type with adhesive on one side only, and adjust the iron to a low-heat setting. If necessary, you can raise the heat a little until the two fabrics bond well. When machine stitching metallics, use a ballpoint needle size 70–80 (10–12), or a size 90–100 (14–16) for the coarse threads. Set the top tension at medium, and use a matching cotton or polyester thread on the bobbin.

Novelty fabrics and materials In this category are many exotic and unusual fabrics with colours, patterns and textures that can produce dramatic effects in a crazy patchwork project. Among these are acetate, plastic, net, fake fur, glitzy and tufted fabrics.

Fake fur with a good high pile can be fun, particularly if it is to be used to make something, such as a cushion (pillow) for a child. Cut out a motif, say a cat or teddy bear, and appliqué it to a random cut patch. Then, using sharp-pointed scissors, trim into shape. Do this carefully, taking care not to shear off too much at first – it cannot be put back!

Washing and ironing is not recommended for many of the novelty fabrics, so the golden rule is to test before use. Many of this group can be dry-cleaned, should it be necessary, while others can usually be refreshed with a clean, slightly damp cloth.

Silks Silk is a unique and exceptional fabric. Silk fibre is amazingly strong, and pure silk fabrics are available in a wide range of weaves, weights and textures – habutai, taffeta, noil, jacquard, twill, dupion, chiffon, velvet, satin and many more. Depending on the type and weave, finishes vary from matt to shiny, and from smooth to coarse. Shot silk is particularly attractive, its two-tone effect resulting from the (horizontal) weft yarn being woven across a warp yarn of a different colour. (The warp is vertical, running parallel to the selvedge of the fabric.) There are also combination fabrics, such as silk/cotton and silk/metallic mixtures, which can be used to good effect in crazy patchwork.

Habutai and pongee are inexpensive and good value. They are widely used for dyeing and painting and come in several different weights and widths. Hand-wash only. Silk noil is an attractive rough-textured silk which is very popular for embroidery and fashion garments. It does not crease easily.

Luxurious chiffons and other silk fabrics dye well, and can be painted and stencilled. Plain silks are often 'weighted' with chemicals and should

A variety of beautiful silks, velvets and brocades similar to those used in working early crazy patchwork.

Metallic, leather and glitzy fabrics combine wonderfully with other fabrics selected for crazy patches.

A collection of silk ties

therefore be washed before any colour is applied. Silk velvet, which has a silk backing and a viscose pile, also dyes well.

While working with silk is always a pleasure, avoid having to unpick a stitched seam, as this can all too easily spoil the fabric. Some silks have a tendency to fade. To combat this, there is an American product called Quilt Guard, which protects wall hangings from UV rays, as well as from dust and stains.

Synthetics A large and interesting range of fabrics comes under this heading – polyester, nylon, viscose and stretch fabrics. All are worth experimenting with, as most of them can be used for making

A fascinating collection of found objects, which includes a butterfly made from fish scales, a beaded snake, shells from a favourite beach, an old photograph and other small mementos.

A collection of soft adornments includes lace motifs, tiny roses, silk flowers, doyleys, silk Valentines, tassels, cords, bows, rosettes, and more …

crazy patches, appliqué or trimmings. Test synthetics for washability, as well as for ironing — some will melt at the sight of the iron.

Woollens Woollen fabrics range from the very fine wool crepe and challis used for dressmaking, to the heavier weights used for suits, coats and blankets. They should be dry-cleaned, as most types of pure woollen fabrics can felt and shrink when wet, and over-handling can cause them to pill. Nevertheless, many types of woollen fabric can be used for crazy patchwork to make a shawl, skirt, car rug or a splendid winter quilt. Iron woollens using a low setting, placing the fabric under a damp cloth to press seams, smooth out creases, or to form a fold-line or an intended crease.

FILLINGS AND BATTINGS

Use polyester toy filling for trapunto (stuffed quilting), and for padding appliqué, and polyester

or cotton batting, available in different weights and widths, for standard quilting. Polyester battings and fillings are washable, but not all the cotton battings wash well. Silk fillings and battings are the ultimate in natural luxury, but rather expensive. They are very soft and make fine fillings for silk appliqué and silk trapunto. Two weights are available and both can be purchased in 40cm and 60cm (16in and 24in) squares.

Use yarns and threads of the appropriate colours for filling the channels of Italian (corded) quilting. Their weight and thickness will be governed by the width of the channel formed by the stitching.

FUSIBLE BONDING FABRICS

Fusible fabrics are used very successfully as a foundation for crazy patchwork. There are several brands of excellent 'iron-on' bonding fabrics that cover a multitude of situations (see also pages 87–9). These versatile products range from the very fine and ultra-soft types, which will give body to delicate fabrics, to the heavier pelmet (valance) weight used to support thicker, stouter fabrics. The stretch type will stabilize stretch and knitted fabrics. The paper-backed form is ideal for quick appliqué, cut-out motifs being bonded to the background fabric. Fusible fabrics are sold in different widths, in white, grey and black. While almost all types are washable and dry-cleanable, it is always safer to test before use.

Particularly useful for crazy patchwork is Filmoplast. This is a self-adhesive distortion-free embroidery backer, designed for machine-sewing. Filmoplast also makes an excellent foundation for backing crazy leather patches prior to stitching. The patches are cut out and simply pressed firmly onto the sticky side of the Filmoplast, abutting each other.

SOURCES OF FABRICS

Quilting specialists and furnishing and department stores are good reliable places to start when buying basic fabrics for a collection. There is a wide choice of current stock and most of the stores will sell short lengths for crazy patchwork. Watch out for their seasonal sales. However, economy is all-important when building up a large and interesting assortment of fabrics. The most likely and rewarding sources are the following: stores selling discontinued lines and ends of rolls, car-boot (garage) sales, country bazaars, auction rooms (for good-quality older and antique fabrics), charity (thrift) shops and, of course, family and friends.

The charity stores almost always have a large selection of fine old silk and polyester ties (see page 18). These are inexpensive, and can easily be recycled into wonderful waistcoats. Simply unpick the ties and store them flat, washing or cleaning and ironing them before use. The design on woven polyester ties is often reversed on the back, providing a choice of two fabrics for the price of one. A novel effect is created when both sides are worked into the same project.

DECORATIONS AND EMBELLISHMENTS

This could be a very long list indeed; however, the earnest crazy patchworker could do no better than to start a good hoard of 'findings' and found objects. Look out for unusual buttons, necklaces, small pieces of jewellery, trinkets, charms, pearls, old earrings and any ornamentation. Charity stores, flea markets and antique malls are all good starting points. For the 'soft stuff', look out for commercially made appliqué motifs, tiny roses, old pieces of lace, doyleys, silk Valentines, embroidered handkerchiefs, tassels, cords, small pieces of needlepoint, painted fabric pictures, and more …

GENERAL EQUIPMENT

In addition to a wide range of fabrics and embellishments, you will require few tools and very little in the way of special equipment. Crazy patchwork is not necessarily an expensive pastime and most of the items listed will already be part of the needleworker's repertoire. Requirements for implementing particular methods and techniques are suggested in the appropriate chapters. Other useful items are listed below.

- Small boxes for storing beads and decorating 'hardware'
- Plastic pattern film, card, paper, scissors, pencil, marker, ruler, tape measure – all in case a pattern has to be made, although this is seldom necessary
- A large basket for storing fabric scraps
- Rotary cutter and board
- Embroidery hoop or frame
- Iron and ironing board

For machine-sewing

Sewing machine (with the appropriate maker's hand-book)
- Machine embroidery hoop
- Presser feet and attachments
- Oil can
- Spare light bulbs
- Practice cloths
- Firm table

PATCHWORK PROJECTS

Crazy patchwork can be used for a huge variety of textile projects. A large range of commercially produced paper patterns for garments, fashion accessories and soft furnishings is available internationally. Styles and designs are very up-to-the-minute. The patterns are simple to follow, and can be easily adapted to suit all tastes.

Chapter Three
METHODS –
VICTORIAN STYLES

Victorian crazy patchwork is recognizable by the quality and quantity of its intricate embroideries and bold embellishments. Exponents took great pains to plan and execute their work artistically yet economically. They would choose randomly cut patches of luxurious velvets, silks and brocades, and apply them to a firm, stabilizing foundation, such as good parts of discarded garments or household linens. The Victorian method of crazy patchwork allowed for great versatility in the shapes and sizes of patches. Patterns and templates were not used, patches being freely cut in asymmetrical shapes and stitched to a foundation to fit in with adjoining patches. It was a haphazard and unconventional method, but it eliminated the anxiety of having to ensure that patches and designs matched up. With almost every scrap being usable, there was virtually no waste.

The edges of soft cotton patches are turned under and basted to a calico foundation, but the seams are not stitched since the embroidery secures the patches. Sequins and an appliquéd flower are added. (Patchwork by Hazel Shell)

This crazy patchwork panel, measuring 25 x 33cm (10 x 13in), was made from luxurious fabrics – silks, satins, brocades and metallics. It is made in the style of much of the Victorian work, the patches being added where required to cover the foundation, as well as the previous seams. Most of the final layer of patches have had all their edges turned under, basted and hand-stitched, so the patching resembles appliqué. The frayed edges of one or two patches add extra texture, and the sides are bound with black satin ribbon. Beautifully embroidered seams hold the piece together. (Panel by Anna Donovan)

THE PATCHES

With the absence of templates, every crazy patch cut has its individual size and shape; it is unmatched. With few exceptions, patches are not necessarily cut out in advance, since identical shapes are seldom required. Because of this, stockpiling patches may not be an advantage, as each one is cut as required to fit a particular space.

Overlapping edges

In early work the edges were not turned under; the raw edges overlapping those of the previous patch. The security of the patches was dependent on the embroidery, which was stitched along the seams and taken through to the foundation. This avoided lumpy seams, but the possible unravelling of raw edges had to be dealt with.

Fortunately, a great many fabrics are sufficiently soft and pliable to have their edges turned under satisfactorily. However, only the overlapping edge of a patch is turned under. The underlying edge lies flat, so that there will only be three layers of patching fabric at the seams. With 6mm (1/4in) turned under along the overlapping edge(s), the patch is first basted in place on the foundation. It then relies on the ensuing seam embroidery (by hand or by machine) for its permanency.

Hand embroidery can be lavish, bold and very attractive, although the stitches must be close enough to avoid gaps along the edge of the seam. Working the seams with machine-stitched fancy patterns, on the other hand, is rapid and effective. While modern

Above: Diagram of sample opposite showing patches with one overlapping edge only turned under and basted.

A small panel, measuring 26.5 x 33cm (10½ x 13in), was made from brilliant brocades, metallics, silk and glitzy fabrics. The patches, with overlapping edges turned under, were stitched to a foundation. Several patches appear to be appliquéd. A machined feather stitch is worked in black shiny rayon thread throughout.

(Panel by Anna Donovan)

machines have a very varied selection of attractive and interesting stitches, the uniformity and regimented appearance of machine stitchery does not appeal to everyone. In the machine-stitched panel shown above, some of the patching resembles appliqué, being similar in this respect to much of the Victorian crazy patchwork. The patches, with all their edges turned under, appear to be simply laid down and stitched in place. Black thread was used to feather stitch along the seams.

There are occasions when bulky fabrics are required for a special project. As these do not turn under easily, you can revert to the earlier method and simply lap the raw edge of each new patch onto the raw edge of the previous patch, basting patches into place prior to stitching. Should the edges of heavier or piled fabrics be likely to fray noticeably, run a very thin line of fabric adhesive or specially made fray-checking product along the wrong side of the patch before basting it in place to overlap a previous patch. It is advisable to machine along the seams of bulky fabrics, using a 'jeans' needle.

Abutting edges

If a really flat, ridge-free seam is desired, abut the two raw edges and lightly glue or baste them to the foundation. They can be made more secure, prior to embroidery, by machine zigzag stitching with monofilament thread. The stitching should be just wide enough to cover and closely unite the two raw edges. Subsequent hand or machine embroidery will further mask the joins.

When piecing leather patches, press them to a (non-iron) fusible foundation, abutting the edges, and then machine zigzag stitch them together.

Using fusible fabrics

Iron-on fusible fabric (see pages 87–9) eliminates the need to turn edges under on individual patches, and at the same time checks fraying. Fusible fabric may also be used as a foundation for patches, as for the silver hat featured opposite. In this case, the patches were ironed directly onto the fusible fabric, cutting out the basting stage. The edges can be either abutted together or overlap other patches, ready for either hand or machine seam embroidery.

PIECING THE PATCHES

Having decided on a project and prepared its foundation, assemble a collection of fabrics. Consider their suitability for the project as regards colour, texture and weight. Remember to allow an extra 6mm ($^1/_4$in) for turnings or overlaps. The first patch should be basted in place on the foundation, with one edge overlapping the seam line by 12mm ($^1/_2$in).

The position of the first patch is not crucial. For a centre start, for example, a three-, four- or five-sided patch is stitched to the foundation, and further patches are added around it in a similar style to log cabin piecing. Each new patch is stitched to the previous patch(es) with right sides facing. The new patch is then brought back over the foundation, and the seam ironed. The next patch is stitched in the same way.

For a corner start, try using a four-sided patch, as for *My Paradise Garden* (see page 27). Add patches in a fan-like manner, outwards and downwards. All subsequent patches are pinned in place, not basted, to allow them to be manoeuvred and rearranged into an acceptable layout. The second patch is cut to fit beside the first patch, overlapping it by 6mm ($^1/_4$in). For the third patch, lay a piece of fabric over the irregular gap to be covered; cut it out, making the patch 6mm ($^1/_4$in) larger all around than the space, and pin it in position.

Continue arranging and pinning patches in random shapes and sizes until the foundation is attractively covered, and the overall composition amalgamates. There is seldom any problem in placing the patches; mistakes are hard to make, and a 'rogue' patch can soon be disguised. Baste to secure the work during the stages of embellishment. Consider incorporating several rounded patches in the piece. Victorian needlework books stress the attractiveness of using curved seams in crazy patchwork, as rounded outlines help to soften the overall effect of a work composed largely of geometric shapes.

Arrange patches at the edges of a block to overlap the seam line by 12mm ($^1/_2$in) in order to ensure that no frayed edges are omitted from the seam. After stitching, the seam allowance should be trimmed back to 6mm ($^1/_4$in) for low-fray fabrics, and to 12mm ($^1/_2$in) for loosely woven fabrics. Oversew the edges by hand or machine to prevent further fraying.

Make a single 20cm (8in) square block as an experiment, and keep a record of the processes. A variety of cushions (pillows), throws or quilts can be produced from a number of blocks. You might try using one block several times over with the same general layout, but each block pieced in different colour combinations, or try rotating successive patched blocks to face in different directions – there are absolutely endless possibilities for experimentation.

The pillbox hat will be in vogue forever; and this vivacious crazy patchwork version will see its wearer through any occasion. Silver-coloured lamé and random-cut patches of metallic fabric, combined with patches of decorative silks in soft blues and greys, are applied to an iron-on fusible foundation. This gives the fabrics body, and helps to control fraying. The hat is stiffened with pelmet- (valance-) weight fabric. A filled tubular ribbon is couched by hand with silver herringbone stitch around every patch. Blue, silver and grey beads, sequins and drops are added at intersections and within some of the patches. A strip of blue silk is gathered to fit the crown, and matches the lining and the lower edges. The hat is trimmed with padded pompoms made from the patching fabrics. Spirals are made by threading craft wire through lengths of tubular rayon ribbon and twisting them for effect. So as not to pierce it, the wire is folded with the looped end taken through the ribbon.
(Hat by Anne Hulbert)

For this cushion (pillow) front, measuring 46cm (18in) square, random-cut patches of hand-dyed velvets and metallic fabric are machined to a foundation using the 'stitch-and-flip' method. The machine embroidery is minimal – any more would detract from the beauty of the colours of these lovely fabrics. (Cushion front by Sandra Wyman)

Full of interest, this colourful crazy patchwork silk panel, measuring 42cm (16¹/₂in) square, is well embellished with a fascinating assortment of gardening memorabilia. It consists of a wide range of random-cut patches of various silks, including habutai, tussore, dupion, shantung, wild and shot types. The patches are stitched to a calico foundation. Hand embroidery, with silk and metallic threads, appliqué, quilting, ribbon embroidery, trapunto and beadwork, decorate the seams and patches. Among the many treasures are silver butterflies, cabochon stars, silk tassels, a silver spider's web, French knot apples, a 'sun' button, glass bead grapes and leaves, a fat bird eating cherries and a 3-dimensional snail. The edges of patches were overlapped and then secured with monofilament stitching prior to embroidery to hold the piecing together during the embroidery stages. While no templates were used for cutting the patches, a plan of the piecing is shown to encourage the newcomer to crazy patchwork.

(My Paradise Garden by Anne Hulbert)

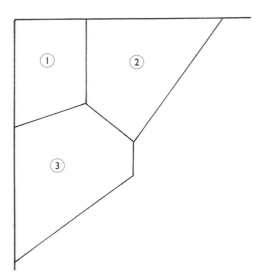

Diagram showing corner start – four-sided patch.

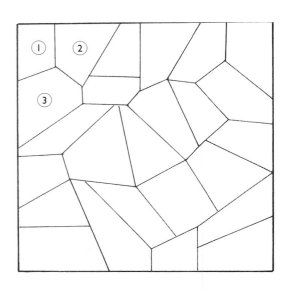

Diagram showing finished layout for My Paradise Garden (see page 27).

A detail of 'Thunderbird' shows contemporary decoration, including crazy patchwork appliquéd to crazy patchwork, pleating, appliqué and raised flowers. The 'feathers' are cut from fabric bonded to a fusible backing, cut out and snipped to make fronds. (Detail from Thunderbird by Delia Salter, see Gallery)

Chapter Four

METHODS –
CRAZY LOG CABIN

Log cabin is a traditional style of patchwork in which parallel strips of fabric are stitched around a central square-shaped patch. It is one of the oldest and best-known forms of piecing. Building up log cabin is easy, and the technique has immense potential. Crazy log cabin patchwork is constructed by the same method as the traditional form – strips round a patch. However, being freely cut, the patches are not squared and the strips (the logs) are not necessarily parallel – nor are there patterns or templates. The

processes are very flexible and adaptable and, as with all crazy patching, each piece of work is unique.

Articles made by the crazy log method are not generally adorned as lavishly as the highly decorated examples of Victorian crazy patchwork. However, simple embroidery and beadwork may enhance the work, and can soften the overall impression of strong lines and sharp angles. There are several examples of crazy log cabin in this book that are attractively decorated with threads and beads.

Diagrams for making trial block as instructed overleaf

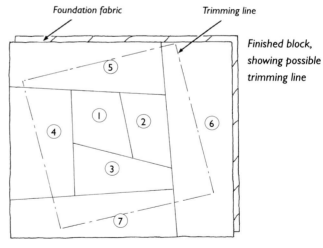

Foundation fabric

Trimming line

Finished block, showing possible trimming line

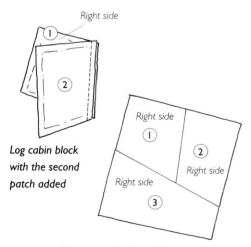

Right side

Log cabin block
with the second
patch added

Right side

Right side

Right side

Three patches in position

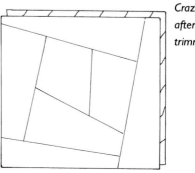

Crazy block
after
trimming

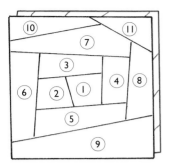 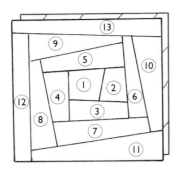 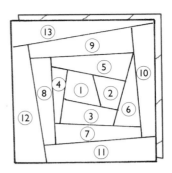 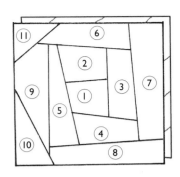

*Four of the blocks of the crazy cushion
(pillow) illustrated below*

METHOD FOR A TRIAL BLOCK (SEE DIAGRAMS ON PAGE 29)

Crazy log cabin patches and logs are stitched to a foundation of calico or other firm fabric. Note that it is necessary to allow 6mm ($1/4$in) extra around each patch for turnings, otherwise the finished block will end up smaller than planned.

- Iron all fabrics to be used.
- Cut out the foundation, making it 21.5cm ($8^{1}/_{2}$in) square, to include 6mm ($1/4$in) turnings.
- Cut out a four-sided 'squarish' starting patch and baste it to the foundation, placing it slightly off centre.
- Cut out the pieces for the sides in a variety of widths – do not attempt to regularize their shapes but be inconsistent, for this is crazy work.
- Cut out the first side patch (2) to fit along one edge of the starting patch (1). With right sides facing, baste and stitch it in place.
- Turn the log (patch 2) over to lie flat on the foundation and iron the seam. Add the next and subsequent logs around the central patch in the same manner.
- Continue until the block is covered, to the point when the last round of side pieces extends beyond the sides of the foundation.
- Baste the edges of the pieced work to the foundation.
- To accentuate the 'craziness', the edges of the finished block can be trimmed at an angle to the original square. In this case, the finished block will be a little smaller than the original.

Random-cut patches make up the intricate designs for the nine blocks and twelve border triangles of this cushion (pillow), measuring 43cm (17in) square. No two are the same. The maker used a very wide assortment of fabrics, colours, prints and textures. When the size of the cushion is taken into account, the tiny size of the pieces becomes apparent – about 185 coloured pieces were used. The cushion is lightly decorated – any more would be 'de trop' – since the fabrics enhance each other. There is an occasional bead and a few shishas were attached with buttonhole stitch. The crazy work is stitched to a foundation. Pieced velvet triangles make up the black areas of the border and the cushion is bound with gold metallic ribbon. (Cushion by Anne Baxter)

The block is now ready to be included as one of many blocks in a large project, such as a quilt, a throw or a cushion (pillow), or used on its own for a pincushion or other small projects.

If a pincushion is to be made, bran or sawdust filling should be used. The cushion casing should be made from a closely woven fabric, such as pillow ticking. Take two squares of fabric, with right sides facing, and stitch around the edges, leaving a gap. Turn the casing right side out; fill until the casing is full and firm, and stitch across the gap. Make the crazy log cabin cover, perhaps using one of the patchwork fabrics for the back; insert the pad, and stitch across the gap. Any embroidery or embellishment must, of course, be added to the log cabin block before the cover is made up.

This completed top for a pincushion is based on a four-sided starting patch. The block is made from cotton and rayon fabrics and is decorated with a few sequins. (Pincushion top by Karen Vickers)

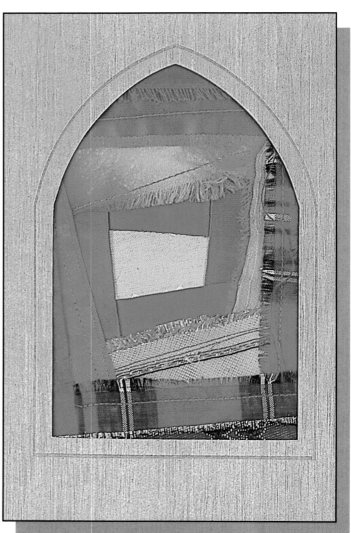

Detail of the randomly cut strips, randomly cut off-centre starting patch and the exotic fabrics that Karen Vickers used for her hanging, Majestic, see Gallery.

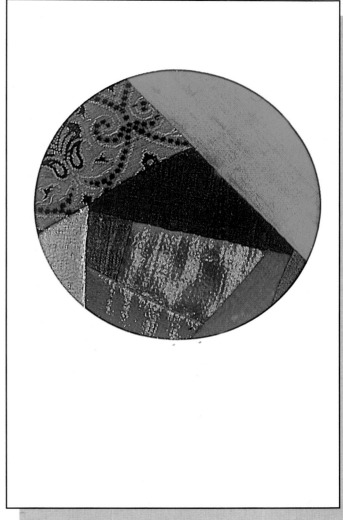

Above and opposite: Four greetings cards with crazy log inserts (note: a range of such cards is available for embroiderers). In each case the piecing was made slightly larger than the opening on the card. A thin line of adhesive was then spread round the edge of the opening at the back, and the patchwork pressed to it. Excess fabric at the back was trimmed off, and the card finished at the back with another piece of card 3mm (8in) smaller all round glued to the back. (Cards by Dorothy Charlton, Moira Low and Karen Vickers)

Chapter Five
METHODS – STITCH-&-FLIP

A further method for applying crazy patches is known as 'stitch-and-flip', or 'sew-and-flip'. Both are contemporary terms for well-tried methods of 'strip piecing', which covers a variety of conventional techniques, including traditional log cabin patchwork. In addition to log cabin blocks, stitch-and-flip is also a widely used and satisfactory method for many other crazy patchwork projects. It offers a fast way of preparing the work for embroidery and further embellishment, added patches being machine-stitched to previously applied patches.

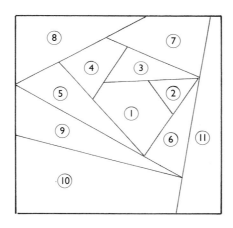

Stitch-and-flip worked around a five-sided patch

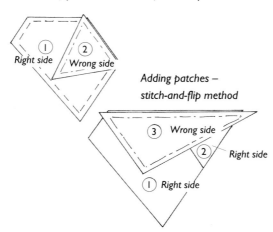

Adding patches –
stitch-and-flip method

'Stitch-and-flip' is worked in the same fashion as log cabin patchwork except that the starting patch can be almost any angular shape, from triangular to eight-sided. The finished piece does not have to be square, added strips can be even more wildly asymmetrical, and the starting patch need not be selected to form the focal point. To create the crazy effect, patches can be cut wedge-shaped, tapering or triangular. The starting patch does not have to be central on the foundation; it can be placed off centre. Often, when required, the shape of the starting patch can determine the ultimate shape of the finished crazy piece.

THE BASIC METHOD

When cutting patches and strips, allow 6mm ($1/4$in) for turnings on all the edges of patches and strips. Cut out the foundation fabric to the required size, again plus turning allowances.

- Cut out and baste a randomly shaped starting patch to the foundation.
- Cut out an irregularly shaped strip and, with right sides facing, stitch it to one side of the patch, and through the foundation. Fold (flip) the strip over onto the foundation and iron the seam.
- Trim the ends of the seam to line up with the central patch and neighbouring edges.
- Continue adding strips around the patch until the project is almost the required size, trimming the ends of each successive seam and ironing the patch flat, before the next strip is added.
- Because of the irregularity of the shapes of the strips, it is very unlikely that they will marry with the edges of the foundation. Add the last round of strips so they overlap the sides. Iron the last seam, turn the work over, right side down, and baste around the edges of the foundation to the overlapping excess. Then, and not before, trim away the excess fabric to make the strips level with the foundation.

*Starting with a four-sided patch, this sample piece,
measuring 27.7cm (11 in) square, was made with
shot silks, dupions and dyed habutai. The machined
seams were trimmed with lace, braid, ruched silk and
thick piping. Machine feather stitching controls the
decorative frayed edges. The block was quilted
through thin batting.*

(By Anne Hulbert)

Glitzy, metallic, brocade, and sequinned synthetic fabrics have been combined here. The resulting piece, measuring 23cm (9in) square, is very similar to the piece on page 35, but was built up around a five-sided starting patch. There are no embellishments, as they could not compete with the fabrics. The block is not padded or quilted.

(By Anne Hulbert)

The stitch-and-flip method is not used only for piecing patches that spiral around a several-sided crazy patch. For instance, randomly cut strips and triangles may be placed horizontally, vertically or diagonally, as shown for the waistcoat on page 37. Indeed, the possible variations of this technique are infinite. It is a very popular method, and well suited to any fabric that will allow edges to be turned without becoming too bulky. Stitch-and-flip has been used for numerous crazy patchwork articles throughout this book.

Detail of a piece of stitch-and-flip crazy patchwork ready to be cut into panels for the silk evening bag shown in the Gallery.
(By Jacqui Wood)

Though not yet completed, this waistcoat is already showing impressive style, with its elegant silk tie fabrics and exuberant embellishments. Gathered and flat variegated tubular ribbons have been couched, and lace ribbon and commercially made motifs appliquéd in position. There are silk thread tassels, a padded appliqué sun, prairie points, gold, cotton and rayon braids – along with bead and sequin embroidery, ribbon embroidery, trapunto (stuffed quilting) and Italian (corded) quilting. Silk, rayon and metallic threads are used for the bold embroidery that decorates the seams. A purchased printed paper pattern was used, the two front pieces being cut out in soft calico (muslin), which served as the foundation fabric for the crazy patchwork. The foundation with patchwork was then made up as one layer of fabric, following the pattern instructions. The crazy piecing was started at one shoulder, the stitch-and-flip method being used to machine-stitch the patches to the foundation. (Waistcoat by Sarah Mitchell)

Also built around a five-sided starting patch, this piece, measuring 27.5cm (11in) square, was made from striped furnishing cotton, the patches all facing in different directions. The patchwork was quilted through one layer of low-loft batting. Again, there are no added embellishments – the arrangement of the stripes is enough.
(By Anne Hulbert)

The patches on this neat panel, measuring 25 x 30cm (10 x 12in) were machined to the foundation around a five-sided starting patch. Furnishing fabrics were used and there is no decoration at all. This design would make an attractive book cover, box lid or cushion (pillow).
(Panel by Mary Lockie)

Chapter Six

METHODS – CRAZY STRIPS PATCHWORK

Asymmetrically cut strips of fabric are among the most versatile of the crazy shapes used for patchwork. It is very easy to select a range of fabrics, cut them directly into an assortment of 'strip' shapes, and then sew the strips together again to create a haphazard arrangement. With this method, it takes little time to produce an original design that has more movement in it than one with parallel lines only. The irregularly shaped strips can be long, short, wide, narrow, tapered or slightly curved. The sides are seldom parallel.

While crazy strips can be sewn to a foundation using the quick and easy stitch-and-flip method (see Chapter 5), there is another method: the cut strips can be bonded to a foundation of iron-on fusible interfacing with the edges abutting together. This avoids lumpy seams and will check fraying. In either case, the seams can afterwards be decorated with hand or machine embroidery.

SUGGESTIONS FOR CRAZY STRIPS

- A simple band or border of crazy strip patchwork is attractive and straightforward to make. Strips of irregular shapes and sizes are stitched together until the band is the required length (A). The uneven edges are then trimmed to the required width and the band is ready for use (B).
- A piece of crazy strip patchwork can be used either as a background on which to appliqué a motif cut from a very different fabric, or as a fabric from which to cut motifs to be applied

(A) Working a crazy strip band

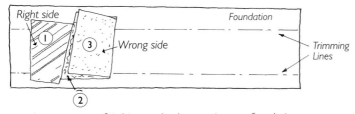

Stitching randomly cut strips to a foundation

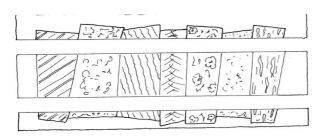

(B) Finished crazy band

(C) Uses for a made-up piece of crazy strip patchwork

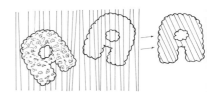

Motif applied to crazy strip patchwork or motif for appliqué cut from crazy strip patchwork

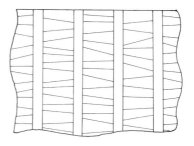

(D) Crazy strips joined by straight sashing

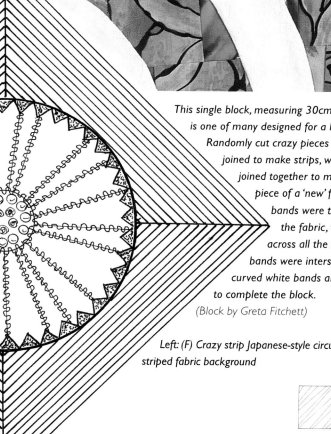

to another fabric (C). Crazy strips can also be joined to make long strips and then made into a quilt with alternate straight sashing strips between the crazy ones (D).

- Another use for crazy strip patchwork is to make several simple blocks – say, some with crazy wavy strips and others with crazy 'straight' strips. They can then be cut and reassembled in different ways to produce borders, or groups of four blocks can be joined together to make a cushion (pillow) (E).

- Fan motifs for appliqué can be made from asymmetrical tapering strips; fans of this type were worked on Victorian crazy patchwork quilts.

- A circle of tapering crazy strips appliquéd to a mitred striped background makes up the striking panel design seen below (F). Hand-embroidery decorates the seams, with French knots and small beads in the centre. The circle is edged with fine braid.

- A striped crazy strip border (G, overleaf) on which half the asymmetrical triangles are cut with stripes running vertically, and the rest with stripes running horizontally. The border design can also be cut into four pieces, reassembled and perhaps used to make a cushion (pillow), as shown overleaf. No attempt should be made to match up the triangles; this would be impossible and in any event would spoil the 'craziness'.

This single block, measuring 30cm (12in) square, is one of many designed for a large quilt. Randomly cut crazy pieces were initially joined to make strips, which were joined together to make a large piece of a 'new' fabric. Curved bands were then cut from the fabric, the cuts running across all the seams. The bands were interspersed with curved white bands and reassembled to complete the block.
(Block by Greta Fitchett)

Left: (F) Crazy strip Japanese-style circular motif set on a striped fabric background

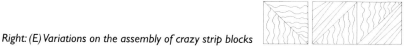
Right: (E) Variations on the assembly of crazy strip blocks

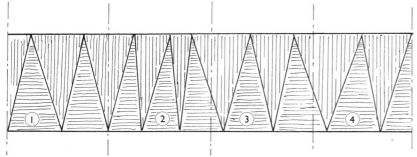

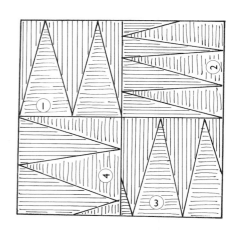

(G) Variations on the assembly of crazy strip blocks

A colourful quilt, measuring 1.4m (55in) square, in the course of being made. The sashings joining the blocks consist of strips cut from a crazy strip patchwork formed from brightly coloured and dark blue randomly cut fabric strips. Each block consists of only four crazy pieces haphazardly cut from an assortment of hand-dyed velvets, silks and metallic fabrics. *(Quilt by Sandra Wyman)*

Freely cut shapes from hand-dyed, tie-dyed and brush-painted strong cottons were worked onto a foundation, measuring 30cm (12in) square. A larger piece of the new fabric thus created would be well suited to covering a contemporary stool or chair seat. (Sample by Hazel Shell)

Left: This vibrant and effective piece of crazy strip patchwork, measuring 51cm (20in) square, was made by first sewing together irregularly shaped strips of fabric to make eight or nine tapering strips with variable numbers of pieces in them. Using the stitch-and-flip method, the strips were then stitched diagonally and in alternate directions, across a foundation.
(Sample by Sheena Henderson)

The seams of this small cushion (pillow) are embellished with hand-stitched embroidery, including herringbone, Cretan and other stitches and their combinations, worked in variegated threads. The cushion cover is finished with an exaggerated border of deep blue velvet. The seams are further decorated with tiny glass and metallic beads, stitched alongside and between the embroidered stitching. Three or four tiny star sequins are stitched at random to each of the pieced strips. The border is decorated with an assortment of sequins, metallic and glass beads, crystals, bugle and metallic and plastic buttons.

(Cushion by Frieda Oxenham)

Chapter Seven

HAND EMBROIDERY – THREADS & TECHNIQUES

Victorian crazy patchwork is identifiable by the abundance of hand-embroidery used to cover the numerous seams, and by the highly decorative areas worked within the silk and velvet patches. However, while the ranges of fabrics, yarns and threads have since widened enormously, embroidery methods and styles have changed very little, and the old techniques remain as popular and fashionable as ever. The range of stitches, and their variations and intricate combinations remain infinite. Being both practical and aesthetic, the seam embroidery joins the patches together and attaches them to the foundation – and at the same time furnishes the work with spectacular decoration.

Among the many ways in which embroidery might be used to embellish the joined patchwork further are the following: stitching single motifs, anchoring found objects, highlighting areas within the patches, monograms, needlepoint and crewel work. Commercially made embroidery transfers are also available in a variety of floral, animal, bird and geometric designs. While transfers are often quite large, components of the pattern can be cut out to make smaller designs for crazy patches. Children's books also provide a useful source of inspiration.

A prodigious collection of hand embroidered work spanning almost 150 years is shown in photographs in this book. These pieces are worthy of close investigation, and a magnifying glass will reveal a wealth of inspiring detail that might otherwise be missed. Study, for example, the hanging *Some Are Borne to Sweet Delight* (see Gallery), which is extensively embroidered by hand.

The crazy log pincushion, measuring 14cm (5¹/₂in) square and made from brilliant silk, rayon, cotton and metallic fabrics has no seam embellishment. Instead, the patches have frayed edges as an alternative to turnings. Stitches include couching, feather, fly, herringbone, satin and stem worked in bright rayon threads.

(Pincushion by Karen Vickers)

Randomly cut strips of silk and wide ribbons provide the background for a range of basic stitches with interesting variations. The imaginative use of threads and yarns, narrow ribbon, tubular rayon, cords and couching are demonstrated. Embroidery threads include silks, rayons, perlés, cottons and metallics. The sampler, measuring 30 x 23cm (12 x 9in), is further decorated with beads, bugles, pearls, cabochons, sequins, buttons and tiny tassels.
(Sampler by Sarah Mitchell)

COMPENDIUM OF EMBROIDERY STITCHES

The following glossary includes 35 basic embroidery stitches, with instructions for working them. These are among the stitches that are most commonly used for crazy work. Experiment with them, combining different stitches to create varied textures and effects, or to add extra dimensions to your designs. Incorporate ribbons, beads, sequins, buttons, findings and other ornamentation to further enhance the richness of beautiful fabrics, or to create an original work of art.

Backstitch

Bring the needle through on the stitch line. Take a small backward stitch through the fabric. Bring the needle through again just in front of the first stitch. Take another backward stitch, inserting the needle at the point at which it first emerged.

Blanket and buttonhole stitches

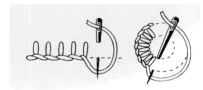

While these stitches are worked in the same way, buttonhole stitches are worked close together. In each case, bring the thread out on the lower line; insert the needle in position on the upper line, taking a straight downward stitch, with the thread under the needle point. Pull up the stitch to form a loop and repeat.

Bullion stitch

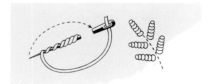

Pick up a backstitch, the size of bullion stitch required. Bring the needle point out where it first emerged, but do not pull the needle right through the fabric. Twist the thread round the needle point as many times as required to equal the space of the back stitch. Hold the left thumb on coiled thread and pull the needle through. Still holding the coiled thread, turn the needle back to where it was inserted (see arrow), and insert it in same place. Pull the thread through until the bullion stitch lies flat. Use a needle with a small eye to allow the thread to pass through the coils easily.

Cable stitch

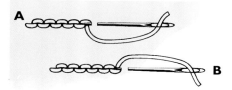

Worked from left to right. A: Bring thread through on the line of design. Insert the needle a little to the right on the line of design and bring it out to the left, midway along the length of the stitch, with the thread below the needle. B: Work the next stitch in the same way, but with the thread above the needle. Continue in this way, alternating the position of the thread.

Chain stitch

Bring the thread out at the top of the line and hold it down with the left thumb. Insert the needle where it last emerged and bring the point out a short distance away. Pull the thread through, keeping the working thread under the needle point.

Chequered chain stitch

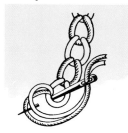

This stitch is worked in the same way as chain stitch, but with two contrasting threads in the needle at the same time. When making loops, place one colour under the needle point and let the other colour lie on top. Pull through both threads. Work the next loop with the other colour under the needle point.

Chevron stitch

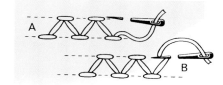

Bring the needle up through the lower line at the left side; insert it a little to the right on the same line and take a small stitch to the left, emerging half-way between the stitch being made. Insert the needle on the upper line a little to the right and make a small stitch to the left, as shown (A).

Next, insert the needle again on the same line a little to the right (B) and take a small stitch to the left, emerging at the centre. Work in this way alternately on upper and lower lines.

Closed feather stitch

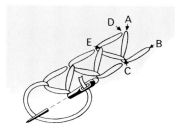

This is worked along two parallel lines. Bring the thread through at A and, with the thread under the needle, take a stitch from B to C. Swing the thread over to the left and, with the thread under the needle, take a stitch from D to E. Repeat these two stages.

Couching

Lay a thread along the line of the design and, with another thread, fasten it down at regular intervals with a small stitch into the fabric. The fastening stitch can be of a contrasting colour to the laid thread. This is a very effective way of fastening down thick and textured decorative yarns.

Cretan stitch

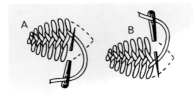

Bring the needle through centrally at the left-hand side, taking a small stitch on the lower line, with the needle pointing inwards and with the thread under the needle point (see A).

Now take a stitch on the upper line, with the thread under the needle (see B). Continue in this way until the shape is filled.

Cross stitch

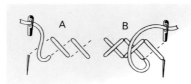

Bring the needle through on the lower right of the intended cross and insert it at the top left of same line, taking a stitch through the fabric to the lower left of the next cross in the line. Continue to the end of the row in this way (A).

Complete the other half of the cross. It is important that the upper half of each stitch lies in the same direction (B).

Double back stitch or closed herringbone

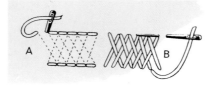

This is used for shadow work on semi-transparent fabric and worked on the right side of fabric as at A. Make small backstitches alternately on each side of marked parallel lines (dotted lines show the formation of thread on the wrong side of fabric). The thread colour appears delicately through sheer fabric.

B shows a closed herringbone stitching on wrong side of fabric, with no spaces left between stitches.

Feather stitch & double feather stitch

For feather stitch (A), bring the thread through at the top centre, and hold the thread down with the left thumb. Insert the needle to the right on the same level and take a small stitch to the centre, keeping the thread under the needle point. Next, insert the needle a little to the left, again on the same level, and take a stitch to the centre, keeping the thread under the point of the needle. Work these two stages alternately.

For double feather stitch (B), two stitches are taken to the right and left alternately.

Fern stitch

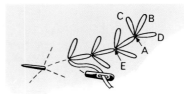

This consists of three straight stitches of equal length radiating from the same central point – A. Bring the thread through at A and make a straight stitch down to B. Bring the thread out again at A and make another straight stitch down to C. Repeat once more at D and bring the thread out at E to commence the next radiating stitches. The central stitch follows the line of the design.

Fishbone

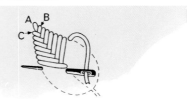

Fishbone and the accompanying open fishbone stitch are both useful filling stitches. For fishbone stitch, bring the thread up through the fabric at A and make a small stitch down the centre line of the shape.

Ribbon stitch

Mark a short line on the fabric and bring the needle and ribbon through to the front at one end. Lay the ribbon flat along the line and gently take the needle back through the fabric, halfway along the ribbon. This forms a fold and loop – an attractive petal shape for daisy-type flowers.

Ribbon weaving

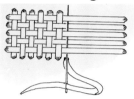

Ribbon weaving can be used to produce a basket effect for flowers, or to fill an outlined area. To work a simple basket effect, first mark the outline for the basket weaving. Bring the needle and ribbon from the back of the fabric through to the front, leaving a 6mm (¹/₄in) end. Keeping the ribbon flat, take the needle directly to the opposite side and through to the back again. Cut off the ribbon, also leaving a 6mm (¹/₄in) end. Slipstitch the ends to the back of the fabric to secure them. Continue attaching strips of ribbon and stitching them to the back of the fabric, keeping them flat, not overlapping. Add the strips in the opposite direction in the same way, also flat and not overlapping. These must be interwoven over and under the first layer of strips, and stitched to the fabric at the back. Use different colours or different widths of ribbon to vary the effect.

Ruching

A simple gathered trim is made by running a gathering thread along the centre of a length of ribbon and drawing it up. This ruching can be varied by adding a narrower ribbon along the centre, or by first stitching together two ribbons of different widths.

Shell-edged ruching

In another variation on ruching, a pretty shell-edged trimming can be made by stitching a gathering thread along the ribbon in a zigzag fashion and drawing it up.

Straight stitch

A simple straight stitch is very useful for stalks and single leaves, for filling a shape or for adding texture to a geometric design.

A three-stranded plait

A three-stranded plait requires three ribbons of equal width and weight. Pin three ends together firmly to a stable work surface, or use a weight to hold them down. Bring the left-hand ribbon over the centre ribbon. Bring the right-hand ribbon over the left-hand ribbon (which is now the centre ribbon). Bring the left-hand ribbon over the right-hand ribbon (now the centre ribbon). Repeat the plaiting – right over left and left over right – until the plait is the required length.

Tubular motif

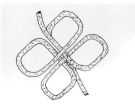

One way to use tubular ribbon is to twist it into a four-looped motif and couch it to the fabric. The motif can be made into a more solid shape by couching more loops inside the outline.

A 'wound around' flower

To make a 'wound around' flower or rose, stitch along a length of ribbon, at the same time drawing it up, and winding it round, with the beginning always in the centre. Baste it to hold the rounds together. Another way is to stitch the starting end in position on a crazy patch and wind the ribbon round, stitching it down as the flower progresses.

Yo-yo flower

Wrong side

Right side

Making a yo-yo flower: Cut a circle of wide ribbon twice the desired diameter of the finished yo-yo. Run a gathering round the edge. Draw it up tightly and finish off securely. To fill out the yo-yo, insert a little stuffing just before finishing the stitching. For a flower centre, make a much smaller yo-yo and stitch it to the centre of the larger one.

ChapterTen

BEAD EMBROIDERY

Bead embroidery, employing every possible style and method, has been the mainstay of embellishment for garments and parlour accessories for centuries, and beads, in every size, shape and colour, have been a component of thread and yarn embroidery for just as long. When Victorian needlewomen took to crazy patchwork as an exciting, new and free form of sewing, they were soon at work making tea-cosies, cushions (pillows), and covers for footstools from randomly cut pieces, and they lavished beads on their creations. Beadwork, however, was seldom used to decorate

American crazy patchwork quilts made in the late 19th century. Not only would beads have added excessive weight to a bed-cover, but a phenomenal quantity would have been required, and it would have taken an incredible time to sew them on.

Nowadays, beads are used freely to highlight modern crazy patchwork, quilting and embroidery. Beads add interest and texture, and glamour too, with their sparkle and colour. They can be couched around the edges of the patches; they may be stitched to lace motifs to pick out the pattern; sometimes they are added to flower centres instead of French knots, and they can be closely sewn directly to a patch to form

Numerous examples of beadwork are used for this sampler, which measures 23 x 19cm (9 x 7 1/2in). They include stitching, threading and couching glass, china and wooden beads, bugles, drops, crystals, sequins and buttons. 'Victorian', 'Edwardian' and contemporary beads are all incorporated. The addition of beads to commercially-made braids, ribbons and appliqué motifs is also demonstrated. There are tiny bugles, as well as very long ones, glass 'leaf' beads, star and dome crystals (cabochon), sequin butterflies, small leaves and a large leaf. The pink pearl cluster is a 1930s earring, and the turquoise 'daisies' were rescued from an old necklace. The ground fabric is a pale mustard linen. After the top row had been worked, the rest was unplanned, following the dictates of mood and the material to hand.
(Bead sampler by Anne Hulbert)

Beaded motifs

flowers and leaves. Beads can also be randomly stitched to patches within crazy blocks, and added to embroidery to highlight the stitches. Anyone who tries their hand at ornamenting with beads will surely fall under their spell.

Beads can be sewn into patterns, used to highlight printed motifs, or to form the eyes of birds, animals and figures. Many of the smaller beads are sold in sizes. Rocailles (little china beads), for instance, come in sizes 8, 10 and others – the higher the number, the smaller the bead. The number denotes the size of the hole, thus governing the size of needle required. It should be remembered that beads may be slightly irregular in size and shape. While this implies that perfectly uniform and symmetrical work may not always be attainable, this is not necessarily a disadvantage. Slight irregularities are a feature of handwork and add to its attraction.

Keep a collection of beads of every possible type, and add to it whenever there is an opportunity. There are excellent specialist shops selling every conceivable variety. Most craft stores also stock the regular sizes, shapes and colours, but look round charity (thrift) shops for any that could be a little more unusual. Beads and findings culled by dismantling old necklaces and bracelets will reap rewards. Occasionally one is fortunate enough to come across a bead-embroidered dress or blouse. Store beads in (lidded) glass jars or in one of those mini chests-of-drawers designed for storing nails and screws.

EQUIPMENT

Very little specialist equipment is required for bead embroidery, much of it being part of the standard embroidery kit:

Beading needles – made for very small beads. They come in sizes 10 to 15 (the finest, for threading tiny beads). Standard sewing needles will often be fine enough for securing larger beads. After prolonged use, a long beading needle becomes quite bowed (though this can be useful for gathering up tiny beads).

Embroidery frame – optional. Remember that a frame can leave ring marks and that it is not always possible to iron the finished work.

Needle-threader – usually necessary for threading tiny eyes.

Scissors – small and sharp-pointed embroidery scissors.

Seam unpicker
Small pliers – used instead of fingers for drawing the needle and thread out of a bead and fabric if they are jammed – it is less painful.
Soft craft wire – used to apply curved beads and bugles.

THREADS
Always use the strongest possible thread, which should be one that can be passed, doubled, through the needle eye and the bead comfortably – often twice, to secure the bead firmly. Be cautious about waxing thread for fine bead embroidery as it may leave a mark on the fabric.

Match the thread to the bead and/or the fabric, depending on which is most likely to show, bearing in mind that the stitching thread may be concealed, particularly if the bead is a bugle.

Button and linen threads These are the strongest threads and should be used with the larger, heavier beads and large-eyed needles.
Nylon This is also very strong, but it can be stretchy, difficult to use and very hard to knot.
Polyester A pure polyester thread, which is fine, tough and strong, and available in practically every shade, is adequate for sewing small beads onto a fabric ground.
Silk Silk thread is strong, but unless it is to be used decoratively, its use could be extravagant.
Wire Occasionally a wire 'thread' might be required; say, to attach a longish curved bugle to a patch, as in the *My Paradise Garden* panel (see page 27). Either fuse wire or soft craft wire work very well. Simply bring the wire through to the front, take through the bead and bring it through to the back again. Twist the ends together so the bead is firmly

A detail from 'Some are Born to Sweet Delight' displays the extent of the hand embroidery, the range of sizes of beads used and the form of the design in only one corner of the quilt.
(By Freda Oxenham)

Beaded motifs

attached and oversew them to the foundation. Trim the ends to about 2.5cm (1in), and cover them with a piece of sticking plaster to prevent them from piercing the fabric, or the fingers.

ATTACHING BEADS

Beads and stitched embroidery make excellent companions. If a patch is to be embroidered as well as beaded, it is generally best to complete the embroidery first. There can be havoc if the embroidery is worked after the beading, because threads and yarns will repeatedly catch round and round the beads, which is irritating and time-wasting. In any case, if you complete the embroidery first, you will be able to scrutinize your work and decide exactly where to place your beads to complement the embroidery.

Having completed any embroidery and selected an appropriate needle and thread for the beadwork, attach the beads as illustrated below. An alternative technique is to add beads as you embroider by picking up a bead on the needle just before it is taken through the fabric to the back and the thread fastened off. To achieve the best results, great accuracy is required in making the stitch and siting the beads correctly.

Stitching a single bead to a patch

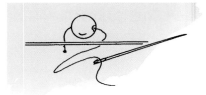

Work a couple of small stitches at the back of the foundation. Bring the needle and thread through to the right side and pick up the bead on the needle. Return the needle through to the back, very close to the hole from which it first emerged – but not through it. Pull the thread gently until the bead lies against the fabric on the front. Repeat this once or twice more to secure the bead firmly. Finish with several stitches in the foundation at the back. Trim off the ends to about 2.5cm (1in). If more beads are to be added nearby, make several stitches at the back of the bead, 'darn' the thread through the foundation fabric to the position for the next bead, and repeat the process.

This crazy log cushion (pillow), measuring 46cm (18in) square, combines randomly cut patches of silk, velvet and printed cotton. The seams were machine-stitched and then beautifully hand-embroidered with a variety of interesting stitches and threads. A very decorative assortment of beads, crystals, sequins and tiny buttons further enhances the work.
(Crazy log cushion by Frieda Oxenham)

Adding a second bead above the first

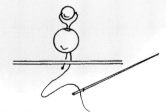

To add a second bead above the first, start stitching the bead as already shown, but pick up a second, smaller bead. Take the thread through this, round and down through the first bead, and through the fabric to the back. If three beads are worked in this fashion, the result becomes a 'drop' or a stalk. This is very effective when glass and china beads, or different shapes of beads are used.

Stitching a rosette

To form a rosette, first mark the outline of the rosette and the centre point on the foundation behind the patch. Bring the needle and thread through to the centre front, pick up a bead and take the needle to the back. Make two or three stitches to anchor it – do not cut the thread.

Stitch a circle of beads around the centre bead, anchoring each one separately as before. Work several rounds until the rosette requires only one more to reach the required size.

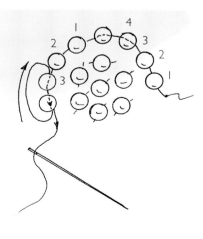

To anchor the final round firmly, use a backstitch technique: bring the needle through to the front, pick up four beads, and then take the needle through to the back. Make a stitch to anchor the beads, and take it through to the front again. Now pick up beads four and three, and then take the needle down between beads two and three, and through to the back again. Continue in this way until the round is completed, anchoring every third and fourth bead in a backstitch fashion.

A rosette can also be made by couching a string of beads to a patch.

Bead filling on a leaf motif

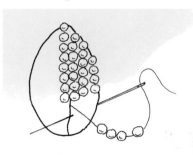

For an effective bead filling on a leaf motif, rows are worked at a slant to give a veined appearance. A slightly raised effect can be made by simply adding an extra bead to each row, but keeping to the original marked outline.

Creating a mound

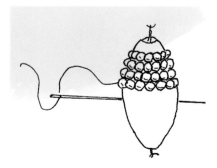

Beads may be stitched over a larger bead to create a mound. Take a larger bead that is flat on one side, and stitch it to the ground fabric. Take the thread with small beads up and over the larger bead and through to the back. Add more, or fewer, beads to follow the shape of the 'mound' bead. Use this technique for flower centres, raised petals and insect bodies.

Couching

Couching a string of threaded beads enables long continuous lines of beads to be stitched into a design. Two needles and thread are used. The first thread (1) is strung with a line of beads. The other thread (2) anchors the string of beads to the fabric. At regular intervals, take the needle (2) over the thread (1), between the beads and catch it to the fabric with a couple of stitches. Small beads only require anchoring to the patch fabric between every two or three beads. Bugles need anchoring with a stitch between each bead to keep them lying flat. The size, shape and order of the beads can be adapted to form many decorative arrangements.

SEQUINS

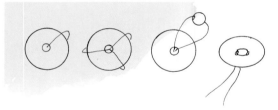

Sequins are almost like confetti. They stick to the fingers and to each other, and they get lost very easily; nevertheless, they are a glorious accompaniment to beadwork and embroidery. The colours can be dazzling, and there is a huge choice of shapes. Fortunately, too, sequins are so incredibly light that they are extremely economical. Most of the simple shapes have one central hole. The larger and more elaborately shaped sequins, such as domes and saucers, have two or more holes.

There are three commonly used methods of sewing a sequin to a patch. The first is to bring the needle to the front and pick up the sequin, and then return the needle to the back again, close to the edge of the sequin.

Another method is to repeat the simple securing stitch twice more, spacing stitches equally. This is more effective if a decorative thread is used.

A feast of glass, china, metallic and wooden beads in an extensive variety of shapes, sizes and colours is available to the embroiderer. There are round, square, oval, tubular (bugle) beads and seed beads in dense and translucent colours. There are also 'jewels', such as cabochon, cut glass, pearls, shisha (little mirrors), and delightfully showy crystals.

Sequins can also be secured with beads. After picking up a sequin, pick up a little bead. Pass the needle back through the sequin before returning it to the back of the patch. Draw the thread through tightly, bringing the bead close against the sequin. Finish with several stitches at the back.

BEADED EDGINGS, DROPS AND FRINGES

It is amazing how differently a drop or tassel can turn out simply by changing the type and style of beads. There are a great many possible variations and the diagrams show just some basic examples. Try out other combinations on a 'doodle cloth' for subsequent reference.

Narrow beaded edge trimmings are very decorative. They can be made from almost any type of bead, but the smaller the beads, the prettier the look. Tiny glass, pearl or china beads, and bugles, can be made into charming trimmings for embroidered crazy patchwork. Narrow edgings do not have to be too elaborate. Simple designs are always appealing – the beauty really lies in the beads.

A single bead edging

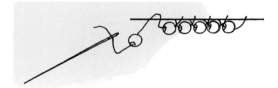

For a single bead edging, the needle is taken through the folded edge of the fabric, through a single bead, and back through the fabric again. The needle must always be taken through the edge of the fabric in the same direction to ensure a uniform finish. As the work progresses, gently pull the thread to keep the beads fairly close to the edge of the fabric.

A two-level bead edging

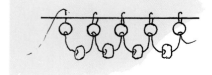

A two-level bead edging is very similar to a single bead one, but with a second 'layer' of beads. After picking up the first bead, the needle is taken down to pick up a second bead. It then picks up a third bead, is taken through the fabric, back through the third bead and down, to repeat the process. The needle must always be taken in the same direction through the fabric.

A looped edging

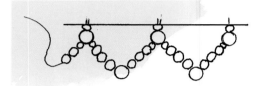

For a looped edging, pick up a small bead with the needle as it leaves the fabric. Next, pick up a large bead, four small beads, a large bead, four small beads, a large bead and a small bead. The needle is then taken through the fabric, down through a small bead, and through a large bead, as shown, to repeat the order of threading to the required length. The number of beads threaded determines the length of the 'fall' and can, of course, be adjusted to suit the piece of work.

A bugle and bead edging

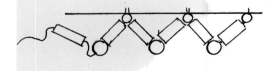

A bugle and bead edging may be made as follows: when the needle leaves the folded fabric edge, it picks up a tiny bead, then a bugle, a tiny bead, a bugle and a tiny bead. The needle is then taken through the edge of the fabric, and back through that tiny bead and a bugle. Continue threading in this order until the required length is reached.

Drops and fringes

Many variations of drops and fringes are possible. A single strand is a drop; a row of single strands, joined to the fabric at the top, becomes a fringe. Early crazy patchworkers decorated small articles, such as

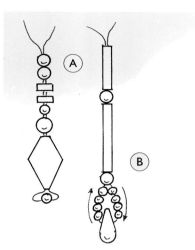

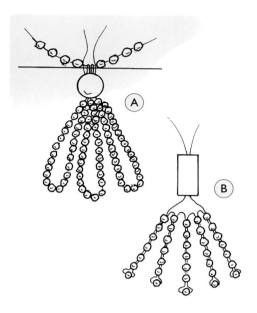

cushions (pillows) and pincushions, with beaded fringes with, perhaps, one or two drops at the corners. A silk lampshade made from crazy patchwork strips and trimmed with a beaded fringe would be magnificent.

For single drop (A), bring the needle out of the fabric to pick up two round beads, two square beads, a small round bead, a larger round bead, a diamond-shaped bead, and a small bead that is larger than the bead above it. Take the needle round the last bead (the 'stop'), back into the diamond bead, and back through all the beads to the fabric again.

Secure the drop with two or three stitches. This can be used as a drop or, by threading more beads, to make a fringe. According to the type and style of beads used, the drop can take on almost any form.

The beads of the second drop (B) are threaded in the same manner as those of the first, but the second drop has a glass pear drop as the 'stop' bead.

If a beaded fringe is to be made, it is of particular importance that the beads on each strand are counted and threaded to maintain uniformity.

Beaded tassels

The looped tassel (A) is the simplest of all and is made as follows: bring the needle through the fabric to the front, and take it through one large bead. Now pick up sufficient smaller beads to form one strand of the tassel loop. To form the loop, take the needle back through the large bead and through the fabric to the back. Fasten off with several small stitches on the foundation. Continue to make further loops of beads as required.

For a tassel of single drops (B), first take the needle through a single bead and continue until seven beads are threaded. The needle is then taken round the seventh, back up through the other six beads, through the fabric to the back and secured to the foundation. Try this with shorter strands, glittery beads, or alternating black and white beads. You could also try putting a sequin between several of the beads.

Chapter Eleven

APPLIQUE

Appliqué is the technique by which a shape (the motif) is cut out from one fabric, laid on another (which forms its new background) and stitched to it. Its main advantage is that it covers an area both quickly and decoratively. The stitching, invisible or visible, can be purely functional, or it can be designed to complement and enhance the character of the design of the motif.

It was an important and popular element in the embellishment of late 19th-century crazy patchwork, being as effective as embroidery. With its ability to enrich an otherwise plain design and add texture and relief, appliqué also has great appeal for contemporary needleworkers. A variety of hand or machine stitches, threads, beads and sequins can be used with advantage to add texture, as well as to highlight the pattern within the motif.

Suggested motifs for appliqué

While the size of a motif for appliqué is of course limited to the area of the patch it is to decorate, its shape has no limitations, and may be abstract, representational or geometric.

When the edges are to be turned under, as was general for basic appliqué before iron-on materials became available, the shapes of motifs are best kept simple: rounded and bold geometric shapes are easiest to manage.

Motifs with more intricate and rugged outlines can nowadays be applied quite easily by using fusible fabrics. Fraying and the need for turnings are avoided, and the motif can be applied quickly and neatly by hand or machine.

Charming motifs can be cut from lace, lace handkerchiefs, damask napkins and doilies and appliquéd to patches of other fabrics. Do not, however, apply a pale lacy cut-out to a pale or printed ground, as the motif will not show up at all. Apply this type of motif to a rich dark ground for maximum effect.

There are also nursery prints galore – covered with lively and colourful animals and figures. A child's bedspread or curtains (drapes) made up from large randomly cut patches with appliqué motifs on them would be impressive, especially if some of the motifs were padded.

FABRICS FOR APPLIQUÉ MOTIFS

While there is a vast assortment of plain and patterned fabrics, the most satisfactory will be those that are closely woven, 'low fray' and of light-to-medium weight. For turned-under edges, fabrics that hold a crease well are an advantage. Most silks and cottons are suitable and easy to manage, as are many rayons and fine woollens. Net, when applied to lie over a printed motif, gives it a misty appearance. Except in special circumstances – perhaps when creating a highly textured project, for example – loosely woven or bulky fabrics, such as tweed, are not altogether suitable. Frayable fabrics can also be a nuisance. In some instances, however, the raw edges

Opposite: The sampler, measuring 23 x 28cm (9 x 11 in), shows a selection of Victorian, Edwardian, art deco and contemporary motifs which could be applied to crazy patches. Included are commercially made, as well as handmade motifs.

(Sampler by Anne Hulbert)

can be left with threads exposed and frayed to create textural interest, and then stitched across to limit the extent of the fraying.

Felt and plastic, and especially the soft and colourful leathers and suedes now available, are ideal for appliqué – no fraying, no turnings, and quick to work. For these materials there is an adhesive 'fabric' onto which the motif is simply pressed very firmly – ironing is not necessary.

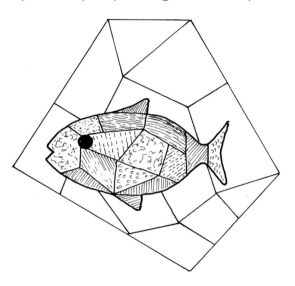

APPLIQUE AND CRAZY PATCHWORK

The techniques of appliqué and crazy patchwork complement each perfectly. There are several ways of combining them. For example, randomly cut patches can be made up to become quite a 'new' and different piece of fabric. Motifs can then be cut out from this and applied to plain or printed patches. Alternatively, they can be cut out and applied to a previously pieced crazy background see illustration above. The 'moose' applied to the border of the *Thunderbird* hanging (see Gallery) is pieced and applied in this way. This method of using crazy patches as an appliqué on a crazy patchwork background can be most effective if contrasting textures, padded patches, or different types of fabrics are used.

Crazy patchwork made from joining random-cut strips together can also be made up into a 'new' fabric. Motifs for appliqué can then be cut from this, or it can be used effectively as a background fabric for plain or patterned crazy patches.

Applying motifs

A decision has to be taken whether to apply motifs before or after the patches are stitched to the foundation. Applying them beforehand is more manageable, as there is only one thickness to work through. Those needlewomen who prefer to complete all the piecing before the appliqué will have to cope with the thickness of the foundation as well as the patch.

Preparing a basic motif

Draw or trace the required motif on the wrong side of the fabric, adding a 6mm ($1/4$in) turning allowance all round, and cut out. Turn the allowance under all around, press, snip curves and baste.

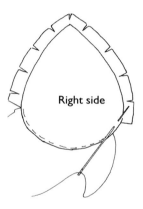

Applying the motif to the background patch

Pin and baste the prepared motif in position on the right side of the cut-out and pressed crazy patch.

Using a small hemstitch or slipstitch, and, if

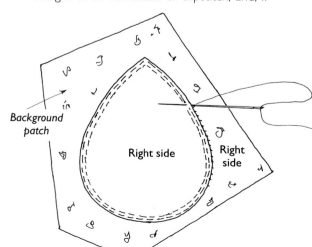

preferred, a matching thread, stitch round the motif to secure. Neat and tidy edges make a good base for beads, buttons, couching and spaced embroidered flowers.

The choice of type and colour of threads for these will depend on the scale of the work, the weight of fabrics and on the desired colour scheme and style. Embroidery on appliqué should be bold and stand out well to compete with other embellishments that may be used to decorate the completed piece of work.

Padding a motif

Extra interest can be given to applied motifs if they are raised slightly by padding. To do this, a little tuft of padding material – cotton or polyester – should be inserted just before the stitching is completed.

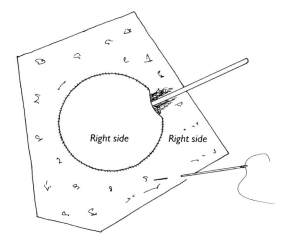

Right side   Right side

USING AN IRON-ON INTERFACING TO BOND A MOTIF

Iron-on fusible interfacing fabrics can be a blessing, especially if you intend to use fabrics, such as lamé or metallic fabric, that have a medium or high risk of fraying. There are types and weights of iron-on fabrics that cover every requirement – standard, firm and heavy, ultra-soft and stretch. A medium-to-lightweight standard fusible fabric is generally suitable for most appliqué techniques.

With many iron-on fusible interfacings, the adhesive is on one side only: the rougher side with a very slight shine. On no account allow the iron to come into contact with this surface, as the sticky adhesive would have to be cleaned off the bottom of the iron.

Using these interfacings eliminates the need to make difficult turnings round the edges of small motifs. Also, without turnings, the bulk is taken out of the edges. Another advantage of most of the fusible fabrics is that the motif design or shape can be traced directly onto the smooth side. Simply lay the interfacing over the drawing, smooth side up, and use it like tracing paper. Remember to check whether or not the tracing of the motif should be reversed to ensure that the motif will be facing the correct way on the patch. Letters and numerals have to be reversed when tracing and marking for application to your chosen background.

Single-sided fusible fabric

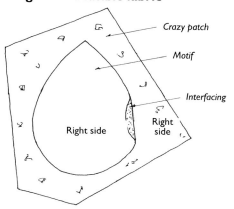

Crazy patch

Motif

Interfacing

Right side   Right side

Use of this material controls fraying so that the edges of the motif need not be turned under. It also permits the insertion of padding from the front, as already shown, or from the back, as in trapunto (see pages 98–9). Single-sided fusible fabrics do not bond the motif to the ground patch, but can help to stabilize delicate fabrics. The motif may be stitched to the patch by hand or machine.

The adhesive side is laid on the wrong side of the motif fabric and bonds to it when ironed. It is important to set the iron temperature correctly to suit the type of fabric used for the motif.

To transfer the design for the appliqué to the fusible fabric, first trace the design for the motif onto the paper, or draw it on the smooth side of the fusible fabric. Cut it out a little larger than marked. If a motif cut from ready-printed fabric is to be used, then a tracing is not necessary. Pin the adhesive surface to the wrong side of the motif fabric and cut out the shape, cutting through both fabrics, along the design outlines.

Baste the motif in position on the right side of the prepared patch.

The motif can now be stitched to the patch by hand or machine, either using decorative hand embroidery stitches or machine fancy stitches.

Double-sided fusible fabric

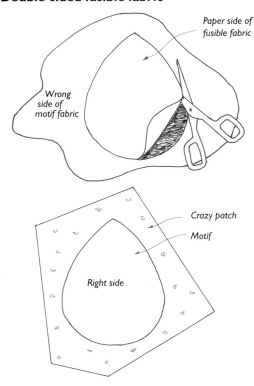

Paper side of fusible fabric

Wrong side of motif fabric

Crazy patch

Motif

Right side

There are also double-sided iron-on fusible fabrics. One side is protected by white paper, which is invaluable for drawings or as a tracing paper. The design can be traced onto the fusible fabric, paper side up, from a drawing or an illustration in a book or magazine. The other side is ironed onto the wrong side of the chosen fabric and the bonded motif is cut out.

The paper is then pulled away, and the motif turned over to lie, right side up (and tacky side down), on the right side of the background (the crazy patch). This method of appliqué does not allow the motif to be padded, as it is closely fused to its background. For this reason too, care must be taken with the choice of the motif fabric – too thin and it might end up looking slightly flat and stiff.

Once the motif is correctly positioned on the fabric, it can be ironed in place. The edges can then be stitched by any method preferred.

USING FREEZER PAPER FOR APPLIQUE

Freezer paper is light and easy to use, and unlike fusible fabrics, is not permanent. It is not adhesive, and the way it is used – by afterwards cutting away the patch and foundation from behind the applied motif – has the added benefit of removing some of the bulk from the crazy patch.

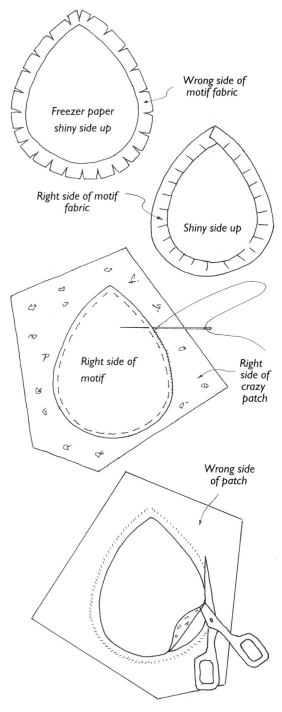

Wrong side of motif fabric

Freezer paper shiny side up

Right side of motif fabric

Shiny side up

Right side of motif

Right side of crazy patch

Wrong side of patch

Suggested motifs for appliqué

First trace, or draw, the motif design onto the paper side of the freezer paper as it is to appear on the front of the patch and then cut it out along the marked line. Lay the fabric to be used for the crazy patch, wrong side up, on the work surface and pin the paper shape to it, with the shiny side up. Cut out the motif fabric, adding 6mm (¹/₄in) all round outside the edge of the paper, and clip curves and corners, as opposite.

Place the motif, with the freezer paper still pinned to it, on a work surface. Carefully fold and iron the seam allowance over onto the shiny area.

Turn the patch over to the right side, remove the pins from the motif and baste and stitch it to the crazy patch. Turn to the back of the work again, and carefully remove the freezer paper from the back of the patch, behind the applied motif, cutting it out 6mm (¹/₄in) inside the line of stitches. Press the work.

STITCHING MOTIFS TO CRAZY PATCHES

The choice of whether to apply a motif by hand or by machine depends on the desired appearance of the finished work, the time it is likely to take, and the convenience, or inconvenience, of machine-stitching.

By hand There are many very decorative stitches that can be used to apply motifs to crazy patches by hand: for example, blanket, cross, feather, herringbone, satin and French knots. The basic techniques, most of which can be combined to achieve a wide variety of effects, are described on pages 46–52.

Should the layers of fabrics (motif, fusible layer, background patch and foundation) feel too thick to stitch through comfortably, then apply each motif to its patch before stitching the latter to its foundation.

Detail of crazy patchwork used as a background for broderie perlé
(by Mary Lockie, see Gallery)

By machine The questions to be considered, if very small motifs are to be applied by machine, are whether it is worth setting up the machine in the first place, and/or whether it will be difficult to manoeuvre the foot and needle round narrow nooks and crannies. A solution to the latter would be to use free-stitching with the feed-dog out of the way.

While a great deal of practice is required to achieve perfection in stitching round the edges of the motif, the results can nevertheless be very impressive.

The sewing machine also has a wide and attractive range of utility and fancy stitches to offer – straight, zigzag, satin, running, blind-stitch, vari-overlock and honeycomb, among others. The manufacturer's handbook will also show how to work several 'by-hand looking' stitches, resembling feather, buttonhole and other hand embroidery stitches.

BRODERIE PERSE

Broderie perse is another kind of appliqué. Traditionally, motifs are cut out from ready-printed fabrics that are commercially made. They are then rearranged into a new design and applied to a different background. Many beautiful fabrics are available, as well as discontinued lines and out-of-date sample books full of wonderful designs. Crazy patchwork makes a particularly attractive background for this method of appliqué.

APPLIQUÉ STEMS, STALKS AND BARS

Being more manipulative than strips of fabric cut along the straight grain, bias-cut strips stretch and ease well for curves and corners. Commercially made bias binding, both plain and printed, and iron-on bias tape are readily available. There are also

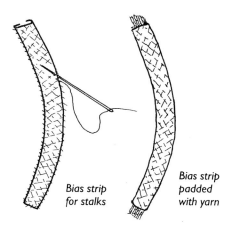

Bias strip for stalks

Bias strip padded with yarn

bias-making gadgets for needleworkers who wish to produce their own. To find the true bias, which is the cross grain of a fabric, take a square of fabric and mark a diagonal line across it from corner to corner. Mark further lines, parallel to the first, to the length and width required, plus 6mm ($^1/_4$in) on each side for turning allowances.

When applying bias strips, iron the turnings under and baste them in position on the patch before slip-stitching the sides to secure them.

To make raised stems, thread a yarn or yarns of an appropriate thickness through the applied strip. Bring the needle and yarn through from the back to the front, take it through the stem and through to the back again. Fasten off the yarn ends, turn the ends of the stem under and slipstitch them to the ground patch so they cover the yarn.

FURTHER SUGGESTIONS

Motifs for appliqué do not always have to be applied to the patch in one piece. Simple shapes, such as the petals of a flower, can be cut out and applied separately, overlapping each other (see diagrams below).

The flower motif can be given another dimension by making a little pleat or tuck as each petal is stitched to the ground patch (see A, B and C below).

Fan motifs were frequently used to enhance early crazy patchwork. They were made from randomly cut sections of scraps of assorted fabrics and were decorated with embroidery, lace and ribbon work. A fan can be any size, ranging from a tiny fan appliquéd to a small patch, to a much larger version spreading across several patches. Stitch the sections together before applying a fan to a small patch. If a large fan is to be worked, then the patches must be joined together before the fan is applied. When made in rich fabrics, fan motifs will always add a touch of luxury to crazy patchwork projects.

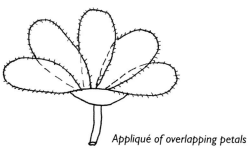

Appliqué of overlapping petals

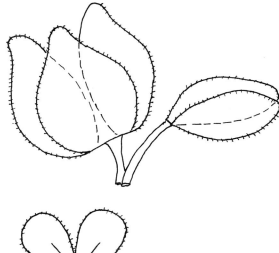

Making a tuck in a petal for a 3-D effect

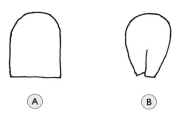

(A)   (B)

(C)

Chapter Twelve

QUILTING IN CRAZY PATCHWORK

Quilting adds a third dimension to an otherwise flat surface by emphasizing certain areas of the design. At the same time, it makes maximum use of light and shade by creating shadows and contrasts between the raised areas and the sunken stitching.

Crazy patchwork and quilting harmonize well, but early crazy patchwork covers were traditionally not quilted. There is little evidence of any padding on the relatively few antique crazy covers that have survived. Victorian women made crazy patchwork covers by stitching randomly cut pieces of fabric in a haphazard fashion directly to a wholecloth foundation.

Towards the end of the 19th century, the crazy-patched tea cosy became very popular as yet another parlour accessory to be shown off. It was, necessarily, very thickly padded and correspondingly weighty. The more superior cosies were richly decorated with beads, embroidery and appliqué, all of which added to the weight.

There are three main forms of quilting – English (wadded), trapunto (stuffed) and Italian (corded). Each of these can look highly effective when worked in the traditional manner on individual crazy patches. These can then be joined into a patchwork in the usual way, offering interesting contrasts with other patches that may be embroidered or embellished in other ways.

All of the quilting methods can easily be adapted to produce very effective and elegant shadow quilting. For this technique, choose a light-coloured semi-transparent fabric for the front top fabric, and a coloured filling. The filling may be a layer of felt for the English method, shredded wool yarns for filling trapunto shapes, and wool or other yarns for

threading for the Italian method. Colours need to be very bright and bold, even gaudy, to show through very fine fabric: it is these bright colours that come through as such soft and beautiful shades.

Each method of quilting can be worked by hand or machine, and is capable of adding interesting contours to almost any size or shape of crazy patch. Designs for quilting can be chosen from a 'doodle' pad, magazines or children's books, and can easily be enlarged or reduced by photocopiers.

All forms of quilting are an asset to crazy patchwork. A single quilted motif worked on an individual patch is very attractive, particularly when interspersed among embroidered or appliquéd patches. Also, try quilting several – say, 15cm (6in) – squares in a variety of techniques and cutting them into several crazy shapes. These can then be pieced together haphazardly to make a sampler or a hanging.

Fabrics and quilting techniques used in the sampler opposite

Note: The chenille* fringe referred to in patch nos. 3, 9 and 30 above can be produced with the tailor tacking foot on many sewing machines.

1 & 25 Randomly stitched lines on polyester satin

2 Italian (corded) quilting on habutai silk

3 Free stitching on cotton furnishing fabric, with chenille* fringed edging

4 Italian (corded) quilting on calico

5 & 11 Trapunto (padded) quilting on silk satin, with metallic threads

6 Random stitching on gold kid leather over thin batting, with metallic threads

7 Italian (corded) quilting, stitched with a double needle on a single layer of stretch velvet

8 & 10 Miscellaneous stitches on calico over batting

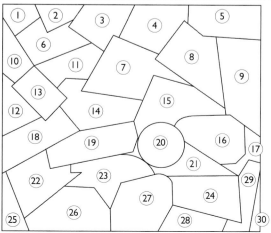

A crazy patchwork sampler, 42 x 38cm (16^1/$_2$ x 15in).
Numerous quilting techniques worked on a range of
fabrics and textures. Crazy patches randomly cut from
previously quilted squares and haphazardly stitched to
a calico foundation, using monofilament thread.
(Sampler by Anne Hulbert)

Left: The diagram and list charts the fabrics, techniques
and threads used for and on each patch.

Randomly cut rectangular and square shapes were joined together and backed with calico, with a layer of batting sandwiched between. The cushion (pillow) front, measuring 30cm (12in) square, is quilted quite haphazardly, using polyester thread and standard straight stitching across the outside shapes. Rayon thread was used for free-stitching embroidery surrounding the applied motif.
(Cushion cover by Greta Fitchett)

9 Chenille* fringing on slubbed silk and batting, using metallic and silk threads
10 as 8
11 as 5
12 Couching on wadded antung silk – rickrack, gold braid, thick wool and silver wire
13 Pintucking and daisy stitching on thickly wadded poly-satin
14 Double needle Italian quilting on soft green leather, with fancy stitches and polyester threads
15 Effective two-way double needle diagonal Italian quilting on striped cotton
16 Shadow trapunto quilting on habutai silk
17 Double needle Italian quilting, cord insert pulled up to ruche fabric
18 Couched braid, ribbon and wool on thickly wadded silk noil
19 Highly raised – 8mm ($^3/_8$in) – trapunto, worked on knitted rayon, outlines double needle stitched, with white filling in two shapes and black filling in the third
20 Even more highly raised – the top fabric was part of a hand-knitted cricket sweater; the stuffed ring is 12mm ($^1/_2$in) high, with solid free-stitching inside

21 Double needle Italian quilting on silk organza; tapestry wool filling
22 Cutwork – layers of black velvet and chiffon, batting and muslin (cheesecloth); areas of the design cut away after stitching the outlines of the design, to leave only the black chiffon
23 Flower on wadded calico – fancy, satin and scallop stitches, with free-stitched infilling
24 Couching on heavy furnishing cotton – thick wools, satin stitched wool, rayon cord and wire braid
25 as 1
26 Couching on lingerie fabric – floss and silk applied with running and scallop stitches
27 Quilted cotton with wadding – honesty pods and leaves are emphasized with free machine embroidery outlines
28 Double needle and straight stitch Italian quilting on heavy dralon
29 Well-raised shadow Italian quilting worked on rayon jersey lingerie fabric
30 Straight stitch Italian quilting on gold leather with metallic chenille* fringe

FABRICS FOR QUILTING

The type of fabric chosen for any form of quilting will determine the actual height of the finished raised design. A stiff fabric will have little 'give', or stretch, whereas a loosely knitted fabric can produce virtual mountains. In between the two, of course, there is a large range of fabrics with a level of 'give' to suit any project.

There are beautiful hand-painted, hand-dyed, commercially printed and stencilled fabrics, as well as some wonderfully textured fabrics.

When cutting out, always cut the layers of fabrics slightly larger than the required finished size. The stitching always takes up the fabric a little, causing some 'shrinking'. This can apply to most quilting, so be warned.

All fabrics should be ironed before use as they cannot be ironed afterwards.

MARKING FABRICS

In this chapter are several collections of drawings suggesting motifs that may be stitched on crazy patchwork, using the various quilting methods. The chosen quilting design is marked on either the front of the top fabric or the outside of the backing fabric,

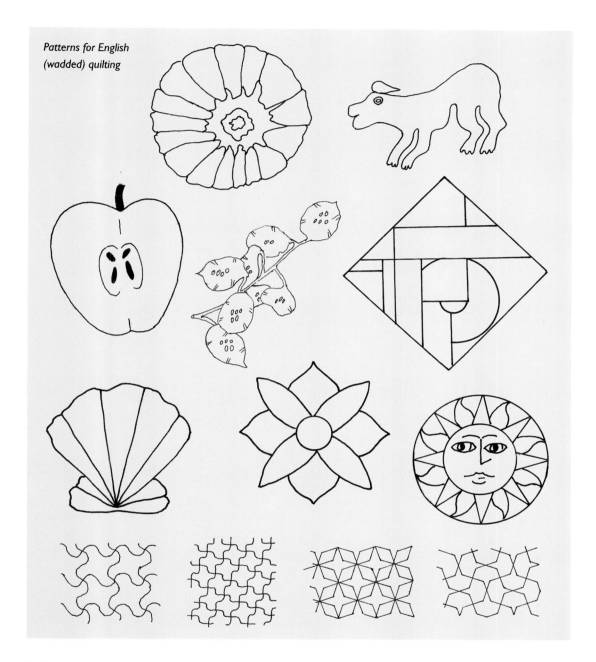

Patterns for English (wadded) quilting

before the two or three layers are basted together. A wide and growing choice of markers is available.

There is no problem if the design is to be marked on the back of the work, for it will be out of sight. The design can be traced through a thin fabric, drawn directly onto a pale backing, or have a paper transfer ironed onto it.

Marking the front of the fabric is a different matter: one must be sure that no marking lines can be seen when the work is finished. Water-soluble pencils and crayons are inexpensive and available in a wide range of colours, and can be used on virtually any colour of fabric. The marked lines of the design can be sponged out after quilting. Ordinary pencils can be used on pale fabrics, but with care. Soft-leaded pencil lines can smudge and are difficult to remove, so hard-leaded pencils are best. An 'H' pencil is usually satisfactory. This makes fine pale lines that may be difficult to see, but which will disappear in the stitching.

Before marking the front or back of the fabric, it must be remembered that in tracing, the image can be reversed. The entire design should always be fully marked out before starting any stitching.

QUILTING MATERIALS AND EQUIPMENT

For most general quilting purposes you will require the following: pencil, ruler, tape measure, scissors, pins, needles, thimble, matching threads, embroidery hoop (optional) and fabric markers or pencils.

Also required are the all-important fabrics for the top/front of the work and the back/foundation, and the correct batting fabrics and filling materials. The latter are referred to on page 20, but in general you will require the battings suggested below:

English quilting Use a 'sheet' form of batting, sold by the metre (yard). Use a thin batting – the aim is to give the work just a slight degree of 'lift' without bulk.

Italian quilting Use quilting wool, or other yarn, thread or cord which can be threaded through the stitched channels easily and effectively.

Trapunto Use synthetic toy or cushion (pillow) filling, sold in bags in ounces or grams.

ENGLISH (WADDED) QUILTING

The English (wadded) method of quilting was the earliest. It was purely functional and used primarily to add warmth and comfort to garments, bedding and floor coverings. The quilting consists of a layer of batting, sandwiched between a layer of backing or lining, and a top layer – the front of the work as shown. Stitching, worked by hand or machine, passes through all the layers, to hold them together and prevent ballooning. The stitching and threads selected can be as quiet or as bold and dramatic as desired to add to the decorative appeal of the work.

The English quilting method can be used to create lovely effects on large crazy patchwork quilts

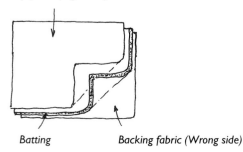

Top fabric (Right side)

Batting   Backing fabric (Wrong side)

and hangings. Patterns can be traditional, geometric or random (see page 95). The additional weight of the batting must be taken into consideration at the planning stage of a project; if the extra layer is too thick, this might inhibit the working of quilting or decorative embroidery by hand.

With the availability of the quilting foot and the walking foot, the sewing machine can, of course, be used to quilt, as well as enrich the work with fancy stitching patterns. A great advantage, too, is its ability to 'free stitch' – with the feed-dog dropped down, or covered. Once mastered, this is a very rapid way of quilting, particularly for making all-over patterns covering large areas (see Machine Embroidery, page 62).

ENGLISH QUILTING ON A CRAZY PATCH

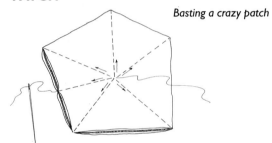

Basting a crazy patch

English (wadded) quilting can easily be worked on a crazy patch. There is an ever-increasing choice of threads to use for both hand- and machine-quilting, including cotton, rayon, metallic and many variegated types. To further enhance the quilting, add a few beads or a little embroidery, and incorporate the quilted crazy patch in the project as desired.

- Mark the outlines of the crazy patch on the front, the batting and the backing fabrics. To each piece, add 6mm ($^1/_4$in) all around for subsequent turnings, and a further 3mm ($^1/_8$in) all round for the slight 'shrinkage', or 'take-up', that the quilting can cause. Cut out all three pieces for the patch.
- Mark the design, with all the lines to be stitched, on the right side of the backing.
- Baste the three layers together as shown. Thread the needle with a thread a few centimetres (inches) longer than the width of the patch. Start stitching at the centre with a knot and baste outwards to the centre of one side. Fasten off.

Below: This ribbon work sampler, measuring 21 x 24cm (8¹/₄ x 9¹/₂in), includes examples of many ribbon work stitches — herringbone, lazy daisy, fern, stem, zigzag, chain, loop, French knots and couching. Also shown are a butterfly bow, roses, rose buds, rosettes, and an iris, a dahlia and a tulip. Ruching, plaiting, prairie points, tassels and pleating have also been worked into the sampler. Beads and sequins add extra sparkle.

(Sampler by Anne Hulbert)

A 'wound around' flower

To make a 'wound around' flower or rose, stitch along a length of ribbon, at the same time drawing it up, and winding it round, with the beginning always in the centre. Baste it to hold the rounds together. Another way is to stitch the starting end in position on a crazy patch and wind the ribbon round, stitching it down as the flower progresses.

Yo-yo flower

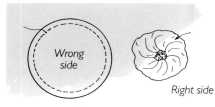

Wrong side

Right side

Making a yo-yo flower: Cut a circle of wide ribbon twice the desired diameter of the finished yo-yo. Run a gathering round the edge. Draw it up tightly and finish off securely. To fill out the yo-yo, insert a little stuffing just before finishing the stitching. For a flower centre, make a much smaller yo-yo and stitch it to the centre of the larger one.

Suggested motifs for appliqué

First trace, or draw, the motif design onto the paper side of the freezer paper as it is to appear on the front of the patch and then cut it out along the marked line. Lay the fabric to be used for the crazy patch, wrong side up, on the work surface and pin the paper shape to it, with the shiny side up. Cut out the motif fabric, adding 6mm ($^1/_4$in) all round outside the edge of the paper, and clip curves and corners, as opposite.

Place the motif, with the freezer paper still pinned to it, on a work surface. Carefully fold and iron the seam allowance over onto the shiny area.

Turn the patch over to the right side, remove the pins from the motif and baste and stitch it to the crazy patch. Turn to the back of the work again, and carefully remove the freezer paper from the back of the patch, behind the applied motif, cutting it out 6mm ($^1/_4$in) inside the line of stitches. Press the work.

STITCHING MOTIFS TO CRAZY PATCHES

The choice of whether to apply a motif by hand or by machine depends on the desired appearance of the finished work, the time it is likely to take, and the convenience, or inconvenience, of machine-stitching.

By hand There are many very decorative stitches that can be used to apply motifs to crazy patches by hand: for example, blanket, cross, feather, herringbone, satin and French knots. The basic techniques, most of which can be combined to achieve a wide variety of effects, are described on pages 46–52.

Should the layers of fabrics (motif, fusible layer, background patch and foundation) feel too thick to stitch through comfortably, then apply each motif to its patch before stitching the latter to its foundation.

Detail of crazy patchwork used as a background for broderie perlé
(by Mary Lockie, see Gallery)

By machine The questions to be considered, if very small motifs are to be applied by machine, are whether it is worth setting up the machine in the first place, and/or whether it will be difficult to manoeuvre the foot and needle round narrow nooks and crannies. A solution to the latter would be to use free-stitching with the feed-dog out of the way.

While a great deal of practice is required to achieve perfection in stitching round the edges of the motif, the results can nevertheless be very impressive.

The sewing machine also has a wide and attractive range of utility and fancy stitches to offer – straight, zigzag, satin, running, blind-stitch, vari-overlock and honeycomb, among others. The manufacturer's handbook will also show how to work several 'by-hand looking' stitches, resembling feather, buttonhole and other hand embroidery stitches.

BRODERIE PERSE

Broderie perse is another kind of appliqué. Traditionally, motifs are cut out from ready-printed fabrics that are commercially made. They are then rearranged into a new design and applied to a different background. Many beautiful fabrics are available, as well as discontinued lines and out-of-date sample books full of wonderful designs. Crazy patchwork makes a particularly attractive background for this method of appliqué.

APPLIQUÉ STEMS, STALKS AND BARS

Being more manipulative than strips of fabric cut along the straight grain, bias-cut strips stretch and ease well for curves and corners. Commercially made bias binding, both plain and printed, and iron-on bias tape are readily available. There are also

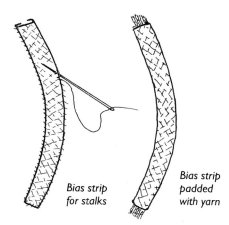

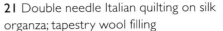

Patterns for English (wadded) quilting

before the two or three layers are basted together. A wide and growing choice of markers is available.

There is no problem if the design is to be marked on the back of the work, for it will be out of sight. The design can be traced through a thin fabric, drawn directly onto a pale backing, or have a paper transfer ironed onto it.

Marking the front of the fabric is a different matter: one must be sure that no marking lines can be seen when the work is finished. Water-soluble pencils and crayons are inexpensive and available in

a wide range of colours, and can be used on virtually any colour of fabric. The marked lines of the design can be sponged out after quilting. Ordinary pencils can be used on pale fabrics, but with care. Soft-leaded pencil lines can smudge and are difficult to remove, so hard-leaded pencils are best. An 'H' pencil is usually satisfactory. This makes fine pale lines that may be difficult to see, but which will disappear in the stitching.

Before marking the front or back of the fabric, it must be remembered that in tracing, the image

This piece of quilted crazy patchwork was made up by joining tiny random-cut silk patches. It was then cut into small squares and triangles and applied to a ground fabric backed with batting. Straight stitches were worked through coloured nets over the centre spaces. Machine herringbone was used for all the remaining stitching, in threads chosen to match the colours of the patches.
(Sample by Jill Curry)

- Thread the needle with the other end of the thread and baste outwards to the centre of the opposite side. Pull the thread firmly to prevent any movement between the three layers. Complete the basting in this way to the remaining side.
- When stitching the design, always start in the centre and work outwards to avoid puckers forming in the centre of the work. Work from the front, but follow the pattern on the back as a guide.
- If stitching by hand, make small, evenly spaced running stitches of the same length front and back. Continue until the stitching is

completed. Fasten off at the back with a few stitches and remove the basting threads.
- If stitching by machine, a walking foot can be fitted to most machines to be used for quilting designs based on straight lines. The quilting foot has a gauge bar attached, which helps to stitch straight, evenly spaced lines. For more complex designs, work free-stitching with a darning foot. This takes some practice, but stitching the design can be very quick. For machine-quilting, it may be necessary to loosen the top tension a little to discourage puckering on the front, or annoying pleats and tucks appearing in the foundation at the back.

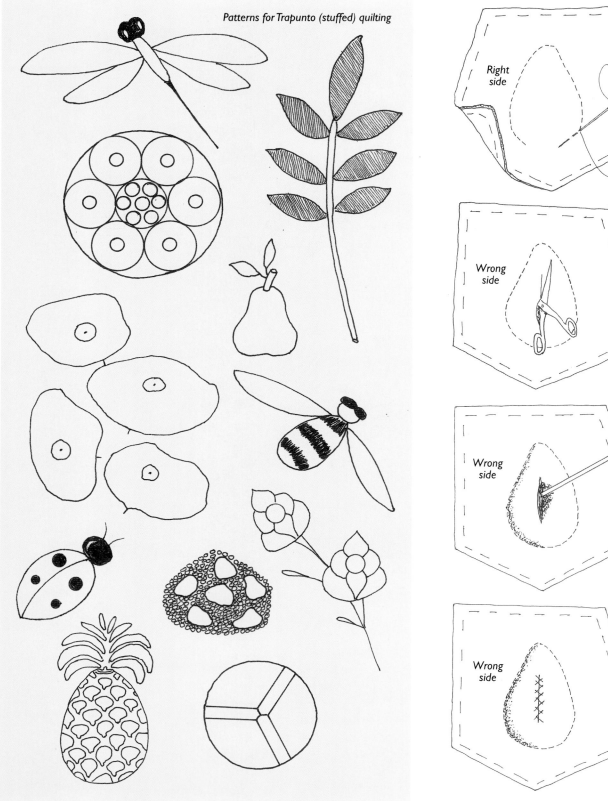

Patterns for Trapunto (stuffed) quilting

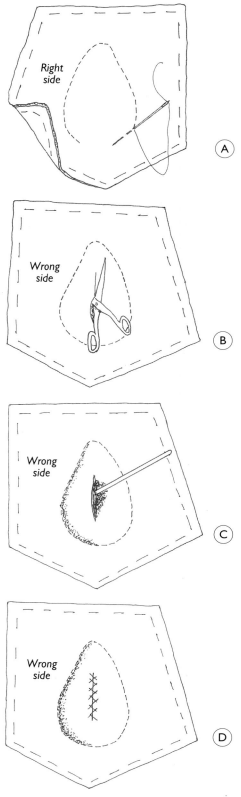

A

B

C

D

Diagrams for working trapunto

TRAPUNTO QUILTING

Trapunto, with its individual raised shapes, is a very satisfactory quilting method with which to highlight patches for crazy patchwork. It may not be the quickest form of quilting, but it is certainly one of the most attractive, producing a considerably greater relief than can be attained using other techniques. Working the softly rounded shapes of trapunto into the same piece as the uniformly raised linear patterns of Italian cording is always attractive, particularly if the cording is stitched across the spaces between the padded shapes.

Trapunto requires only two layers of fabric – the front fabric and the foundation backing. The outlines of the components of the design for raising are stitched through both fabrics. Padding is then inserted into the enclosed areas from the back to give emphasis to the selected shapes. Some examples of patterns for trapunto are shown opposite.

TRAPUNTO ON A CRAZY PATCH

An additional requirement is a stick to use for padding out the shape. Wooden sticks are best as they do not slip about and are easier to control. A wooden cuticle stick, with both a flat end and a slanted end, is ideal. Do not use anything with a pointed end as the point would be sure to pierce the front fabric, spoiling it. Do not use a crochet hook either – after pushing in the filling, its hook will just pull it out again, and the other end will not get into the corners properly. Butchers' wooden skewers are also suitable, but the point must be well rounded off before use (see diagrams opposite).

- Mark the crazy patch on the front of the foundation fabric. Add 6mm ($^1/_4$in) all round for turnings, and a further 3mm ($^1/_8$in) all round for the slight 'shrinkage', or 'take-up' that trapunto quilting can cause. Cut out both pieces of the patch.
- Mark all the areas to be raised on the outside of either the backing or the top fabric.
- Baste the top fabric to the backing, stitching round the edges.
- Stitch, by the preferred method, all round the outlines of the shapes to be raised. Fasten off at the back. It is important that all the stitching is finished before the padding is begun (A in diagram opposite).

Patterns for working Italian (corded) quilting

Diagrams for Italian (corded) quilting

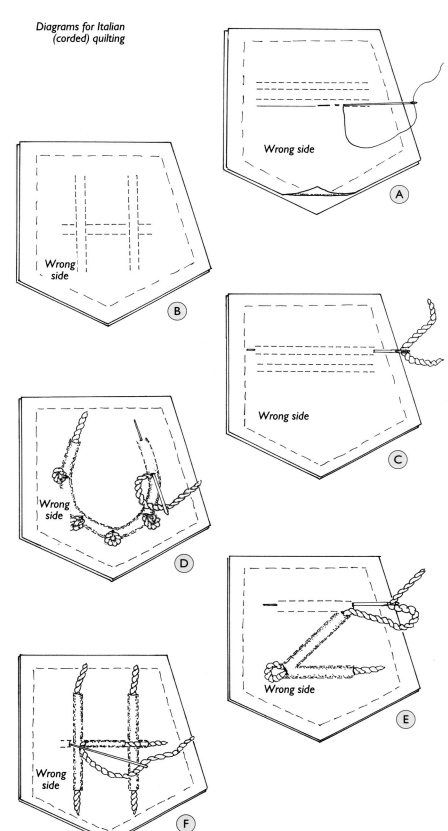

- Cut a short slit, or slits, in the backing behind the shape or shapes. Make these cuts short as the slits can stretch and become difficult to close again after filling (B, on page 98).
- Ease the filling into the shape. Fill the areas furthest from the slit first, and the area of the slit last. Do not overfill or the shape(s) will end up stretched and hard. On the other hand, too little filling will leave empty 'pouches' (C, on page 98).
- When a shape is softly and evenly filled, close the slit with several herringbone stitches (D, on page 98).
- Fill all the shapes in the design to be raised. Add further decoration as required. Sew little beads in the flat areas between the raised shapes, or embroider them with French knots.

When the trapunto is finished, it can be incorporated in the crazy project.

ITALIAN (CORDED) QUILTING

Italian quilting is mainly used for decoration. It somewhat resembles trapunto in that the design is stitched through two fabrics and the filling is inserted after the stitching. It is a very attractive and versatile form of quilting and pairs well with trapunto to create very pleasing effects.

Designs for Italian quilting are based on parallel lines stitched through two layers of fabric to form wide or narrow channels for filling. Thread, yarn or cord of an appropriate thickness is then threaded through the channels to raise the surface.

Although the technique is based on parallel lines, this does not mean that the width of the channels in a piece of work has to be identical. Narrow channels can alternate with wide ones and they can be stitched in curves and circles, or other geometric shapes. The running or back stitches may be made by hand or machine. The latter certainly speeds up the work. Ordinary machine straight stitching, some of the fancy stitches and even the twin needle can all play a part in corded quilting.

The Italian quilting method

An extra requirement for this type of work is a bodkin with a ball-point or rounded end that cannot pierce the front fabric. Several types and lengths are available. The size is governed by the width of the stitched channels through which the threaded bodkin must easily pass.

- Mark the crazy patch outline on the front or the backing fabric. Add 6mm (¹/₄in) all around for turnings, and a further 3mm (¹/₈ in) to allow for the quilting take-up or 'shrinkage'. Cut out both pieces of the patch.
- Mark the pattern lines to be corded on the right side of either the backing or the top fabric.
- Baste the two pieces together, avoiding the quilting channels.
- Stitch by hand, or by machine, along all the marked pairs of parallel lines of the pattern. Complete the stitching before the cording is commenced (A)– see diagram opposite.
- When pairs of channel lines cross at any point in the design, stitch only one pair in continuous lines, leaving the channel open. The other channel lines should run right up to the lines only at either side of the first channel. They must not cross it since it would be impossible to thread the yarn through (B).
- Thread a bodkin with selected yarn. While the yarn must not be too long, it must be sufficiently long to go through the channel with no likelihood of a join inside.
- Slide the bodkin and yarn into a channel, and ease it through to emerge at the other end (C).
- Avoid puckers forming when threading through curved channels in the design. Make tiny snips at regular intervals in the channel at the back. Bring the bodkin out at the first opening, and then re-insert it at the same point, leaving a small loop of yarn. Continue threading yarn

through the channel in this way (D).
- Puckering or tension can be similarly avoided at corners. Bring the bodkin out through a tiny snip at the back of the corner and re-insert it through the same hole, leaving a small loop of yarn at the back. Continue in this way until all the threading is completed (E).
- To thread yarn through crossing lines, first thread the yarn through the continuous channel. Insert the bodkin into the second channel. Bring it out again through a tiny snip in the backing, made at the intersection. Re-insert it at the other side and continue threading it through the channel. Do not pull the yarn within the channels too tightly or the work will pucker (F).
- Whenever the yarn enters or leaves a channel, always leave ends of about 7cm (3in) to allow the work to 'give'. When the quilting is finished, gently pull outwards on the bias from the centre. This will allow the cord to settle and ease any tension within the channels. It will also prevent the cord from later disappearing back inside the channel.

Shadow Italian quilting

This can be very pretty, as can be seen in the crazy patchwork sampler on page 93. Simply use a very pale near-transparent fabric, such as organza or fine habutai silk, for the front, and pick very brightly coloured yarns for filling the channels. The result can be amazing: not at all gaudy as one might expect – just lovely fondant, ice creamy shades. Enhance further with beads, French knots or other embroidery.

Chapter Thirteen

FINISHING TOUCHES

Attention to small details — the finishing touches — can turn even a small sample piece into a work of art. The following are some suggestions for ways in which to enhance your work and to add those little extras that make all the difference.

COLOURING FABRICS

If fabrics are not available in the required shades, or a range of toning fabrics is needed, it is often well worth taking the time and effort to create your own coloured fabrics.

Great artistic skills are not required for colouring fabric. There are no hard and fast rules and previous experience is not necessary. Dyeing, by whatever method, is an inexpensive and effective way of producing special effects on almost any fabric or material. There is a wide choice of dyeing products and equipment, and techniques can often be combined.

The main advantage of colouring fabric for small-scale crazy patchwork is that small areas can be quickly transformed and only correspondingly small quantities of dyes and colouring materials are required. Thus, special patches can be individually coloured prior to further embellishment.

COLOURANTS AND TECHNIQUES

Many fabric colourants are available — follow the individual maker's instructions, as the procedure can vary. Always work on a protected surface, and wear protective gloves and a waterproof apron. Fabrics, paints and dyes (liquids) are intermixable and can be used in a vast number of ways — painting, spattering, splashing and printing. Combining methods can have very decorative results. The following are just some of the techniques worth using for crazy patch fabrics.

- Lovely effects are easily achieved by tie-and-dye techniques, in which fabrics are bound, folded or simply scrunched and tied before being immersed in a liquid dye.

- Fabric pens, crayons and permanent markers are ideal for lettering, outlining and detail work. Pens and markers — particularly the metallic ones — can also be used for writing on fabrics. For either script or marking detail on fabric, place the fabric in an embroidery frame to keep it taut. If a patch is too small to be put into a frame, baste it to a larger piece of fabric and then frame it.

- Stencilling can be done with crayons, with a special brush or by spray-dyeing the fabric. Parchment or card is required for making stencils.

- Transfer paints and crayons are ironed onto the fabric in the same way as an embroidery transfer. The design, which can consist either of outlines or of coloured-in areas, is first drawn or traced on paper, so remember that the image will be reversed when it is ironed on the fabric.

- Very attractive antique-style sepia effects can come from simply using tea or coffee to colour pale cream and off-white fabrics.

- Sponges — either natural or synthetic — may be used to dab fabric with dye. The fabric can look very attractive if several colours are used.

LACING A PANEL OVER CARD

Before framing a piece of work, it should be laced over a firm backing. This will not only ensure that the work is taut and wrinkle-free, but will also give it strength and support. It is necessary for the work to have at least 10cm (4in) of surplus fabric outside the boundaries to provide the necessary wrap-over for the lacing.

You will require a piece of thick card, hardboard or 3-ply cut to the exact size of the finished outer edges of the work; a piece of 50g (2oz) wadding cut 2.5cm (1in) larger all round than the board; pins; a large-eyed needle and strong button thread.

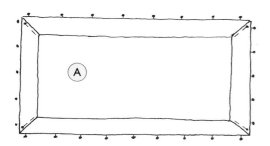

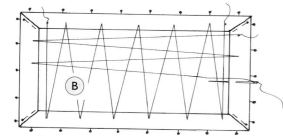

- Lay the work face down. Place the wadding centrally over the back with the board on top. There will be a small surplus of wadding all round which will protect the work from the edges of the board.
- Pull the surplus fabric over to the back and secure with pins into the edges of the board. Start with the bottom and the top, beginning at the centres and working outward to the corners, then pin the sides, always pulling the fabric taut before pinning. Mitre the corners and pin the folds, as shown (A, above).
- Start lacing, first lacing the bottom to the top and then lacing from side to side. Remove any slack in the fabric as lacing progresses (B).
- Stitch the corners. The work is now ready to be framed.

Note: When the work that is to be framed has raised areas, such as beadwork or quilting, the frame must be recessed to prevent the glass from pressing on the work.

TIED QUILTING

Tying is a quick and easy way of finishing a quilt. The technique simply involves tying reef (square) knots through the layers of a quilt to hold them together, and to prevent 'ballooning'. Use a sturdy, non-slippery thread, such as cotton perlé, yarn or crochet cotton. Tying can be worked on the back or the front of the work, and the ends of thread can be fluffed out like little tassels. The intersections of a quilt with joined blocks make suitable positions for the ties.

More decorative ties for quilting in crazy patchwork can be in the form of narrow ribbons, bows, buttons stitched on, tufted ends or tassels.

To make a basic tie

Mark a dot on the quilt where the first knot is to be. Pin through all the layers on the dot. With a threaded needle, make a backstitch over the pin through all layers, leaving an end of about 10cm (4in). Make a second knot over the first and trim the end as the first.
- Tie the thread ends into a reef (square) knot.
- Take the right-hand end of yarn over the left, take it through and pull taut (A, below).
- Take the left-hand end of yarn over the right, take it through and pull both ends taut (B).
- Pull the knot tight, trim the ends and fluff out (C).

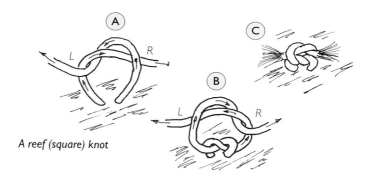

A reef (square) knot

TASSELS

Tassels, perhaps added to the corners of a cushion (pillow) cover, add a touch of luxury to crazy patchwork and they are quick and easy to make. If leftover threads from the project are used, they will match perfectly. They can be made in any size required in a variety of threads – metallics, for example, or bright and shiny rayons, as well as silk ribbons, strips of fabric, leather thonging or pre-twisted cords. Mix thicknesses, textures and colours boldly, but note that the heavier threads will hang down better than very light threads. Many sizes of tassel can be seen within this book.

TO MAKE A SIMPLE 9CM (3¹/₂IN) TASSEL

All that is required for this basic tassel is some firm card, scissors, needle and threads.
- Cut a piece of card 9cm (3¹/₂in) wide.

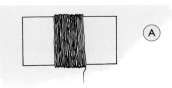

- Wrap the chosen thread round and round the card (A) until it is as thick as required – the more thread, the thicker the tassel.
- Slide the needle with about 46cm (18in) of thread under the wrapped thread at the top. Take it through again and tie the ends tightly together to hold the wrapped threads and to prevent them slipping out. Do not cut off the long ends – they will be required to fasten the top of the tassel to the project (B).

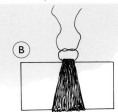

- Cut through the bottom loops of the tassel and remove the card.
- Holding the tassel firmly, wrap a long matching or contrasting thread tightly round the tassel to make the 'neck' (C).

- Take the needle and thread through the tassel several times and under the wrapping to secure. Trim the ends if necessary.

Another type of tassel can be made by passing threads through a bead.
- Tie a knot at each end to hold the bead, and fluff up the ends.

DOLLY TASSELS

Dolly tassels can be made in any size and give a very attractive finishing trim to cushions (pillows), hangings, roller blinds (shades), tote bags and fashion accessories. They can be made in any of a variety of fabrics – silk, cotton, leather, metallic and novelty. Fabrics with a natural firmness are preferable as the dollies will then hold their flaring shape well.

The finished height of a dolly tassel will be just under half the diameter of the circles used. The garden cushion (pillow) (see Projects) has 16 dolly tassels.

For each tassel, you will require two circles of fabric; matching threads; one bead, and ribbon or yarn with which to attach the tassel to the project.
- With right sides facing, stitch the circles together 6mm (¼in) from the edge, leaving a 4cm (1½in) gap for turning.
- Turn right side out, slipstitch across the gap and iron the seam.
- Place the bead at the centre of the inside of the dolly tassel.
- Hold the bead in place and pick up the dolly tassel with the bead inside.
- Take a needle and thread, and make a knot at the end large enough not to slip through the bead.

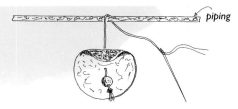
piping

- Pass the needle up through the bead, through the top of the circle and on through a piping seam on the cushion (pillow) or use for another project.
- Wind yarn round and round the dolly tassel, close in against the bead.
- Tie the ends together, pass them under the wound yarn to hide the knot, taking them to the inside of the dolly, and fasten off. Finish stitching the tassel in place.

CRAZY STRIP ROSETTE

This type of rosette consists of randomly cut strips joined together. Scraps left over from a patchwork project can be used, thus ensuring the rosette's compatibility with the fabrics and colours used in the crazy piecing.

A 10cm (4in) diameter rosette

- Cut random strips of fabric about 15cm (6in) long and stitch them together, with right sides facing, to make a band of about 38cm (15in) long. Iron the seams flat open. Trim the sides to make a 10cm (4in) wide band.

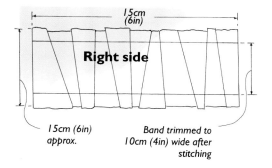

15cm
(6in)

Right side

15cm (6in)
approx.

Band trimmed to
10cm (4in) wide after
stitching

- Stitch the ends together with right sides facing, turn right side out, and fold in half lengthwise to form a ring.

Wrong side

- Run a gathering thread around the raw edges through both layers and pull up tight. Cover the centre with a small pompon or a few beads.

Note: The diameter of a finished rosette will always be the same as the width of the strip-pieced band before it is folded in half.

CORD, BRAIDS AND PIPING

An edging made with a selection of the fabrics and yarns used for the project is the ideal way to make ties, create handles for a bag, finish off a cushion (pillow), chair or footstool cover, or make a border for a small hanging or picture.

TWISTED CORD

There is no magic about making cord quickly and easily. It has many practical and decorative uses – as a simple trimming, looped for a more interesting edging, plaited or couched. Some fascinating and unusual cords can be produced by mixing various types, colours, textures and thicknesses of yarn.

The requirements are plain or mixed yarns at least four times as long as the desired finished cord; a heavy weight or a board with a nail hammered into it, and a pencil.

- Fold the yarns in half and tie the ends together to form a circle.
- Slip the loop end over the fixed nail, or under the weight (for a longer cord, the loop can be fixed around a door handle).
- Slip the pencil through the knotted end. Pull taut and turn the pencil clockwise – twisting the yarns into a cord. Allow the twists to travel along the yarns.
- When the yarns are well twisted, they will kink when loosened slightly.
- Fold the (pencil) knotted end over to the end on the nail. As you do this, the two halves of the cord will quickly twist round each other. Remove from the nail and smooth the finished cord along to ease out any bumpy wrinkles.

MACHINE-WRAPPED YARNS AND CORDS

Yarns that have been wrapped together can be very decorative, particularly when seemingly unlikely types of yarns are combined to make new forms. Interesting examples may be seen on the Barcelona bag on page 67. Yarn/cord-wrapping can be worked using either the darning foot or the braiding foot of the machine.

Using the darning foot

- Fit the darning foot, and take the yarns through the foot to the back, together with the thread ends from the needle and the bobbin.

- Lower the foot. Assess the maximum zigzag width of the needle by turning the flywheel by hand. The needle should just clear the yarns at each side.
- Holding the yarns at the back and at the front, very slowly start stitching. Do not pull the yarns too much, they will just require controlled guiding. It will soon be seen that the cords are being wrapped by the stitching. While this is not difficult to work, practice is required.

Using the braiding foot

The disadvantage of using the braiding foot is the restricted width of the hole, which limits the number and the thickness of yarns to be wrapped. However, fine and silky yarns can be joined together very effectively with this method.

Foot-free cords

Experienced machine embroiderers do not use a foot for yarn-wrapping. Thicker yarns and more of them can be combined, with the stitch width set to its widest for really bulky results. Although no foot is used, the presser foot lever must be lowered to engage the upper tension.

PIPING

Piping is a length of fabric-covered cord that is inserted into a seam to give a neat and attractive finish to an edge. The fabric is generally cut on the bias and the cord can vary in thickness from very fine to thick 'jumbo' types.

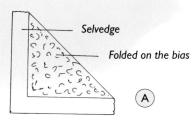

Selvedge

Folded on the bias

(A)

- Fold the fabric to find the bias across the straight grain (A). For the true bias, the fabric

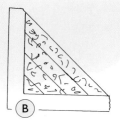

(B)

should be a square. Trim away selvedges before cutting and joining bias strips.
- Mark lines parallel to the fold, as shown, and cut into strips (B). The widths must be the width of the required bias plus 6mm (1/4in) seam allowances on both edges.
- Join the strips, when necessary, as shown (C) to ensure a continuous straight edge over the join. Iron the seams flat and snip off the surplus.
- Fold the fabric lengthwise over the cord and baste through, as close as possible to the cord (D).

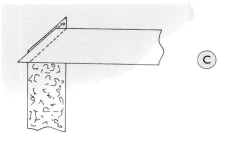

(C)

- Baste the piping onto the right side of the front of the work, as shown. Snip the corners to enable the piping to negotiate the curve (E).

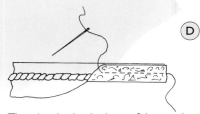

(D)

- Then lay the back piece of the work over the piped top, with right sides facing. Baste and stitch through all layers as close as possible to the enclosed cord.

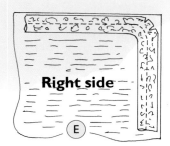

Right side

(E)

An alternative to traditional piping can be made by covering brightly coloured yarn with near-transparent silk. This will produce a soft and pretty shadow effect and enhance a crazy patchwork article.

Glorios by Anne Baxter

A brilliant collection of fabrics, in different colours and textures, was used to create crazy strips, crazy triangles and crazy log cabin for this small hanging, which measures 48 x 50cm (19 x 20in). The size of the work indicates the small scale of most of the random-cut silks and cottons. The work is decorated with hand embroidery, couching and shisha beads. The finishing touches include an interesting variety of handmade tassels of tiny beads and bugles, silken strands with a row of larger tassels of unravelled mixed yarns along the bottom. The hanging is bound with metallic gold ribbon.

Chapter Fourteen

PROJECTS

CHRISTMAS STOCKING
By Mary Lockie

On examination, the patchwork of this stocking really is crazy – oddly shaped patches haphazardly arranged. Several patches have had all the edges turned under and appliquéd to cover the edges of previous patches – hence the diversity of shapes. The stocking is made entirely by machine. Metallic gold embroidery is worked along the seams of the patches. This is a quick, easy and effective method.

The stocking is 38cm (15in) high, 17cm (6¾in) wide at the top and 20cm (8in) from heel to toe.

Materials

Red cotton – 46 × 91cm (18 × 36in) wide for the stocking back, front lining, back lining, cuff back and hanging loop
Green cotton – 23 × 46cm (9 × 18in) for heel, toe and cuff front
An assortment of 'Christmas' printed cottons
Batting (50g/2oz) – 46 × 24cm (18 × 9½in)
Matching threads for making up
Gold metallic embroidery thread

To make

Enlarge the given pattern if it is to be used, or judge the outline and fill in the patch shapes by eye. Make a paper pattern of the stocking outline, adding 6mm (¼in) all round for turnings. Mark round the pattern on red cotton and cut out the three main pieces, then mark round the batting and cut out two pieces.

From green cotton cut out a strip, 10 × 19cm (4 × 7½in), for the cuff and mark and cut out the heel and toe pieces. Baste the outside back and back lining together with one layer of batting sandwiched between. Using red thread, stitch quilting lines, 4cm (1½in) apart, diagonally across the piece. Baste the three layers together across the top; set aside.

Baste the front lining and batting together. Start patching about 9cm (3½in) down from the top, with the batting uppermost. Baste patch 1 to the batting in the position shown – do not fold the turnings under. Turn the left-hand edge of patch 2 and baste it to overlap patch 1. Turn under the left-hand edge of patch 3 and baste it to overlap patch 2. Continue patching down towards the heel and toe, turning under any edges that will overlap previous patches. Baste the heel and toe pieces in place. With patching completed, use gold thread and decorative stitching to embellish the seams. Work satin stitch to apply the heel and toe.

Baste the cuff to the top of the patchwork, right sides facing. Fold it upwards and iron the seam. Work gold stitching along the seam. Baste

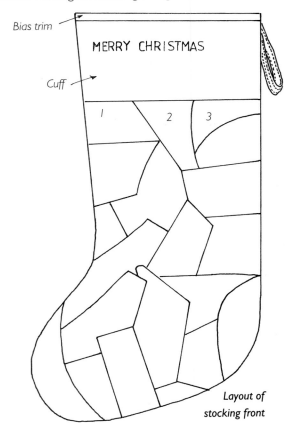

Bias trim

MERRY CHRISTMAS

Cuff

Layout of stocking front

the three layers together across the top. Stitch 'Merry Christmas' on the cuff.

With right sides facing, baste the back and front together round the sides and foot. Neaten the edges with zig-zag or interlocking stitching. Turn right side out. Cut a red strip, 2.5 × 11cm (1 × 4½in), for the loop. Fold into four lengthwise and stitch along both edges. Fold in half and pin the ends at the back seam on the top edge.

For the trim, cut a red cotton bias strip, 2.5 × 37cm (1 × 14½in). Fold under and iron 6mm (¼in) along the sides. Join the ends to make a circle fitting round the stocking top. With right sides facing, stitch the trim to the front of the stocking, ensuring that the ends of the loop are included in the seam. Turn it over to the inside and slipstich. Iron the trim.

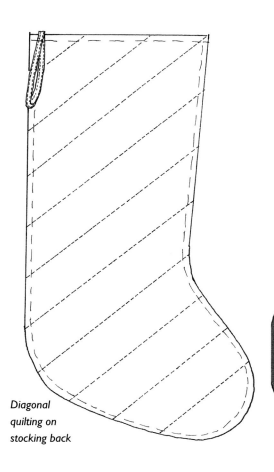

Diagonal quilting on stocking back

SHIFT DRESS
By Sheena Henderson
and Anne Hulbert

Use an 'easy-to-make' commercial pattern to make this pretty voile dress with a crazy patchwork front. Three colourways of the same print are used. The seams joining the patches are embroidered throughout in herringbone stitch using several toning colours of perlé (no. 5) cotton threads.

Cotton perlé has an attractive sheen and slips through the fabric easily and quickly. Paper patterns are available in numerous sizes and give fabric requirements for each size. However, extra fabric will be required for the crazy patchworked front — approximately 60cm (⅝ yd) of each of the three colourways.

Pin the dress front of the paper pattern onto a lightweight lining fabric (this will be the foundation for the patchwork). Cut this out, adding a 2.5cm (1in) extra allowance all round to allow for any 'shrinkage' caused by thread tension during the embroidery.

Cut out several crazy patches. Baste the first patch to the foundation at one shoulder (see A). Turn 6mm (¼in) under the edges of subsequent patches which will overlap previous patches and baste them to the foundation.

Machine zig-zag along the seams using monofilament (invisible) thread (this will check fraying and hold the work together during the stages of the hand embroidery). Work downwards, across the front towards the side, allowing the patches to flow over the front. Avoid centrally placed patches and symmetrical arrangements.

Embroider herringbone stitching along the seams — lengthwise there should be about four 'crosses' to 2.5cm (1in). Stitches 6mm (¼in) wide should cover the monofilament stitching. Mix the colours well, avoiding too many of the same colour in one area.

When the crazy patchwork and the embroidery are complete, as shown in the photograph, trim round the dress front to the correct seam lines. Make up the dress according to the pattern instructions.

This dress would look good made in black with metallic gold embroidery, perhaps as a full length version for evening wear.

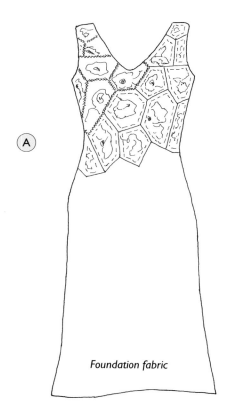

Ⓐ

Foundation fabric

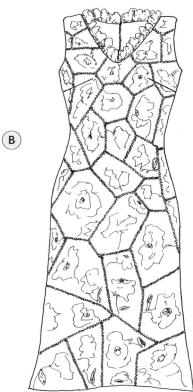

Ⓑ

*Applying crazy patches
to the dress front foundation*

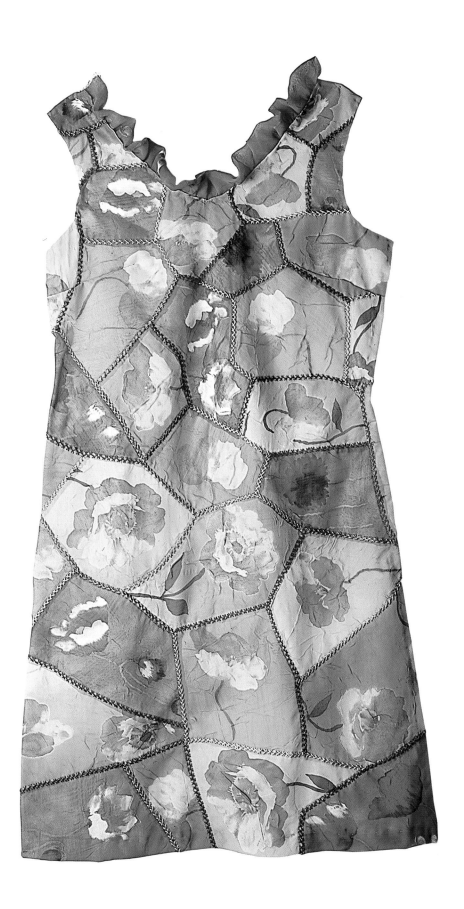

KIMONO
By Celia Eddy

Once Japanese traditional costume, the kimono was adopted by the western world to satisfy fashion trends, particularly for dressing gowns. It is an easy garment to make and crazy strip patchwork is quick to work on the sewing machine. Choose a simple paper pattern with a straight seam running down from the shoulder to the under arm. Silks, satins and velvets are used for this kimono. The foundation is made from a lightweight cotton lawn, while the lining is made in a rich toning satin. The paper patterns will give the quantity of fabrics needed for the required size. However, estimates of the different fabrics required for the patches is difficult: to be on the safe side, collect a sufficient quantity of pieces to cover the foundation at least twice. (Note: Allow for 6mm (¼in) turnings round all sides of the patches.)

Prepare the foundation: Pin the paper pattern sections onto the lawn; cut out the two front sections, the back and the sleeves, adding 2.5cm (1in) all round each piece to allow for stitching, or quilting 'take-up'. Set aside while making the crazy strips. Cut the fabrics into crazy strip shapes. They may be long, short, wide or narrow, and have straight or slanted ends, but should be cut with the sides on the straight of the grain. With right sides facing, stitch the ends of the patches together to form long strips. Iron the seams. Also, with right sides facing, stitch the long strips together lengthwise and iron these seams. The long strips run up and down the garment.

Continue piecing until sufficient length and width of 'fabric' has been worked to cover one section of the foundation. Baste the patchwork, right side up, onto the foundation. Working on the right side, stitch through both layers along the stitched seam lines ('stitching-in-the-ditch') to hold the layers together. Trim to size round the edges. Continue in the same way for the remaining sections of the garment.

Follow the pattern instructions for the lining, collar, cuffs, tie-belt and for making up the kimono. Bands of simple patchwork strips will make attractive cuffs. If required, the kimono may be quilted. In this case, sandwich a layer of batting between the completed patchwork and the foundation. Baste through all layers. Stitch 'in-the-ditch' as before.

Back of kimono

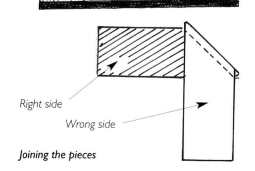

'Stitching-in-the-ditch'

Right side

Wrong side

Joining the pieces

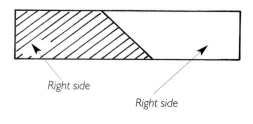

Right side

Right side

Joining the strips

EVENING BAG
By Phyllis Furse

Rich fabrics, including brocade, silk, lace, embroidered net, velvet and satin, were used to make this pretty crazy patchwork evening bag. The lining is purple satin. Purple yarns, tubular ribbons and metallic threads were plaited for the strap. Hand and machine embroidery in a variety of threads, beads and sequins decorate the seams. The side tassels are formed by simply tying the ends of the plait into a thick knot and the bag is fastened with a loop over a bead. A bead motif decorates the flap. There are two pattern pieces – one for the bag front, the other for the back and flap in one piece. The 'stitch-and-flip' method of piecing is used. The bag measures 21 × 23cm (8 × 9in).

Materials

   Firm calico for the foundation – 22 × 24cm (8½ × 9½in) for the front, 22 × 34cm (8½ × 13½in) for the back and flap
   Satin for lining – two pieces cut as for foundations
   Plenty of fabrics for patches – 12 are applied to the front and 18 to the back and flap
   Matching threads for assembling and embroidery threads for decorating seams
   A variety of ribbons, 1.5m (60in) long, for plaiting the strap

The diagram (left) gives the pattern for the bag. The whole shape – AA, BB, C and D – is the back and flap, while the front pattern is the section below the A – A line. Make the two pattern pieces: D – C is 34cm (13½in) ; A – A and B – B are 22cm (8½in) ; and A – A down to C is 24cm (9½in). Mark the identifying letters and cut out. Seam allowances of 6mm (¼in) are included on the main pieces. Mark and cut out the front and back in foundation and lining fabrics. If the given arrangement for the patches is to be used, add 6mm (¼in) turnings all round each one. Start with the bag front. Cut out patch 1 and baste it to the foundation where indicated (B). With right sides facing, baste and stitch patch 2 to patch 1 (see diagram). 'Flip' the patch over onto the foundation and iron the seam. Add patch 3 to 1 and 2 in the same way (see diagram).

Arrangement of patches for front of bag

Inside of flap

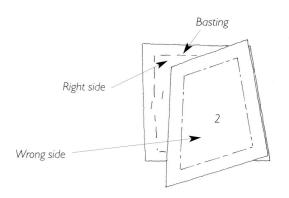

Basting

Right side

Wrong side

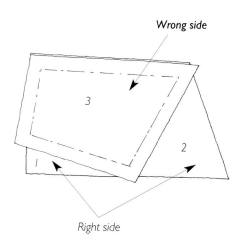

Wrong side

Right side

Continue adding and 'stitching-and-flipping' patches round the centre in the order shown, ending with patch 12.

Apply random-cut crazy patches to the back and flap in the same manner. Using the photograph as a guide, embroider the seams and decorate further with beads and sequins. Sew metallic beads to form the motif on the flap.

Make up the bag: With right sides facing, baste and stitch the pieced bag front to the pieced back, matching AA, BB and CC. Turn right side out. With right sides facing, baste and stitch the two lining pieces together matching AA, BB and CC. Leave inside out. Turn under, iron and baste 6mm (¼in) along the top edge of the front and all round the edge of the flap too. Turn under, iron and baste a slightly wider allowance round the lining edges.

Slip the lining inside the bag, matching AA, BB and CC. Baste the turned edges of the lining 3mm (⅛in) inside the edges of the bag front and flap. Use tiny slip stitches to join them together. Remove the basting threads.

To make the strap, divide sufficient tubular ribbons and yarns into three thickish strands about 1.5m (60in) long and plait (braid) together. Make a knot at each end, leaving 'tails' of about 5cm (2in). Stitch to the bag, just above the knot at X at each side.

For the fastener, stitch a 12mm (½in) bead, with a 12mm (½in) shank to take the loop, as shown on the bag front. Make a chain stitch loop on the flap point to reach over the bead. Add the tassel (see Finishing Touches) to the lower point of the front at X.

Further suggestion: On a much larger scale, this design would make a fine bag in machine-embroidered soft leather or suede.

AFRICAN HAT
By Anne Hulbert

This colourful hat is made from hand-printed cottons collected in South Africa. Though worn by African men, these hats are also reminiscent of Victorian smoking caps. Most manufacturers of paper patterns include easy-to-make 'pillbox'-shaped hats in various sizes.

For the hat shown in the photograph random-cut patches are bonded and machine satin-stitched to a fusible foundation using polyester thread. A variety of random-cut long triangles form the crown. The hat is lined with one of the patching fabrics. It is decorated with groups of small china beads and a tassel to match the lining.

The required fabrics for making both the crown and side band are: firm, iron-on fusible interfacing for the foundations, pelmet-weight (valance-weight) stiffening or buckram, and plenty of printed cotton pieces for patching plus extra for the lining. The pattern will give the quantities for the particular size required.

First, make the crown. Cut out one circle in fusible interfacing for the foundation and one circle in the stiffening. Lay the fusible circle on the work table with the adhesive surface upwards and mark the centre point. From the cottons cut out 12 to 14 triangular shapes to reach from the centre to the edge of the circle, varying their shape and size. Place them on the circle to overlap each other by barely 3mm (⅛in). Iron the patches to secure them to the foundation. Set the machine stitch width to 3½ to 4, and the length to ½ to 0 for satin stitch. Start at one edge and work up and across the centre and down the opposite side to the edge. Baste this pieced circle to the circle of stiffening.

Make the side-band: Cut out the side-band in the stiffener and the fusible (foundation) fabrics. Lay the foundation on the work table with the adhesive side uppermost. From the cottons, cut out one or two irregular, crazy patches. Place the first patch on one end of the band with the raw corner edges overlapping the foundation, as shown in A.

Overlapping edges by barely 3mm (⅛in), add patches 2 and 3 in the positions shown. Carefully iron to bond to the foundation. Continue to add patches, random-cutting, placing, overlapping and bonding as before until the side-band is covered. The patches must always overlap the edges of the foundation to ensure their inclusion in the seams. Set the machine for satin stitch as worked on the

Ⓐ

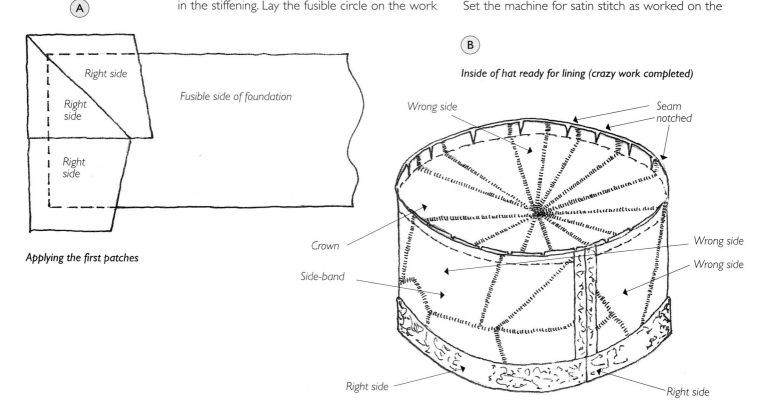

Applying the first patches

Ⓑ

Inside of hat ready for lining (crazy work completed)

crown and stitch round the patches in the same manner until all the edges are covered. Baste the pieced side-band to its band of stiffening.

For making up the hat, assume both the pieced crown and the pieced side-band to be one layer of fabric. Follow the pattern instructions for completing and lining the hat. See also B for the inside of the hat prior to lining. Remember that both the side-band and lining seams must match up and lie at the back.

Decorating the hat: Use coloured china beads, stitching small groups and loops of beads, couched beads and flower forms at intervals round the front. Take the stitches through to the lining to prevent it ballooning. The tassel is made from cotton yarns, as shown in Finishing Touches, or can be bought from craft shops. Attach the loop of the tassel to the centre of the crown and take the stitches through to the lining to prevent it ballooning.

COT COVER
By Anne Hulbert and Audrey Kenny

Plain and printed curved crazy strips of fleece were used for this warm and lightweight cot cover. Fleece fabric is easy to work with since it does not fray and is usually reversible. The cover is made by machine and measures 91 × 137cm (36 × 54in). There are 24 blocks, each 23cm (9in) square (finished), with nine crazy swirls for each block. Turning allowances are not necessary when applying the strips to the foundation squares or when joining the pieced blocks – in both instances the edges must abut each other.

Compressed 85g (3oz) polyester batting ('firm needle wadding') forms the foundation for each block (this type of batting is unlikely to snag in the machine). Red marbled cotton fabric backs the cover and binds the edges. The finished cover is 'tie quilted' at the intersections of the blocks to prevent the layers ballooning.

The block design arose from freely drawing swirled lines across a 23-cm (9-in) square of paper and cutting out the shapes as shown on the layout plan. The haphazard arrangements of plain and printed fleeces ensure that every block is different. Cut out each strip from the fleece fabric as it comes. Over planning and organizing can waste time and fabric, and can spoil the craziness. Do not pick out particular motifs – cutting through them gives more interest to the design.

First, copy, or trace and enlarge, the layout plan onto a 23-cm (9-in) paper square. Number the nine pieces and cut them out. Cut the foundation batting into twenty-four 23-cm (9-in) squares. Mark round the strips on the coloured fleeces and cut them out. Baste strip 1 to one corner, then baste strips 2 to 9 to the batting in the positions shown, making sure that the edges really do abut each other. Set the machine stitch to its widest zigzag and the stitch length to 1½–2. The stitches should be about 5mm ($^3/_{16}$in) apart. Stitch slowly, ensuring that the zigzag stitching falls equally over both edges, securing them to the batting foundation. The stitching will automatically quilt the seams in the block. Piece the remaining blocks in the same manner.

Complete the cover front. Using the same thread and stitch settings, join six blocks together in groups of four, with strip 1 placed in the centre of each group, as shown in the photograph. Cut out the red cotton backing, 91 × 137cm (36 × 54in), to fit the back of the joined blocks. With right side uppermost, baste it in place. For the ends of the cover, cut two bands, each 6.5cm (2½in) wide and 93cm (36½in) long. Turn under and iron 6mm (¼in) along the sides of each band. With right sides facing, baste and stitch one long edge to the front of the cot cover. Fold the band over to the back and slip stitch it to the backing, along the fold. Repeat for the band at the other end. Cut two bands for the sides, each 6.5cm (2½in) wide × 138.5cm (54½in) long. Turn under and iron 6mm (¼in) along each end, and along each side of each band. Baste and stitch as for the cover ends. Slip stitch across the folded gaps at each end. The cot cover is now ready to be 'tie-quilted' (see Finishing Touches).

Layout plan

LARGE TABLECLOTH
By Anne Hulbert and Audrey Kenny

This colourful crazy patchwork tablecloth is 182cm (72in) in diameter. The A to B lengths (see A) are 91cm (36in). It can, however, be made to any size by copying and enlarging the plan for the twenty patches in each panel. The shapes and layout of the patches in each of the six panels are identical, but the fabrics in each are not necessarily so.

The patches are random-cut from furnishing cottons and overlap each other to ensure flat seams. The foundation is cotton lawn and rickrack braid covers all the seams. Monofilament (invisible) thread is used throughout for the stitching, with a no. 30 cotton thread on the bobbin. Opaque template plastic will be required for making the patch templates, whether the given pattern or an original design is used. The patching and the rickrack braiding on the six panels should be completed on their foundations before making up the cloth.

First, copy and enlarge the pattern with the crazy design for one section onto firm paper. On this, mark the number of each patch with its order of application as shown (A). Using the plastic, trace off the template for each patch. Cut out each template 3mm (⅛in) outside the marked edges to allow for overlapping the edges of the patches. Number each template accordingly.

Cut out the six sections in the foundation lawn. Lay one of them on the work table ready to start piecing. Mark round templates 1, 2 and 3 on the wrong side of the fabrics and cut them out. Baste patch 1 in position along the corner edges of the foundation, then baste patch 2 in the position shown, overlapping one edge of patch 1 by 3mm (⅛in). Baste patch 3 in position, overlapping patches 1 and 2 as shown. Continue cutting out and basting patches to the foundation, working down towards the lower edge until the piecing is completed. Iron the work.

Apply the braid, basting measured lengths over the seams joining the patches. Apply in lengths as long as possible. To avoid lumpy joins, slip stitch any ends under adjoining braids. Using monofilament thread, machine zigzag stitching to secure. Baste firmly through the layers – the piecing, the foundation and the braid – along both A to B sides to stabilize all the edges. Trim the edges and

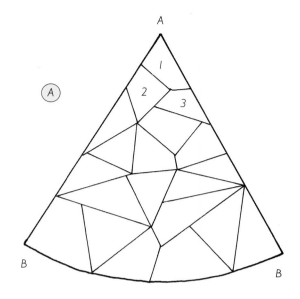

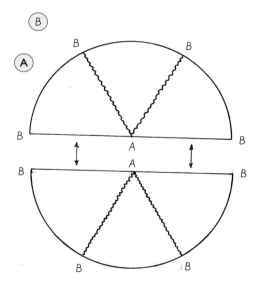

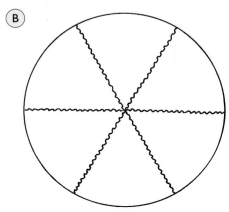

machine zigzag all along to neaten. Complete the remaining five panels in the same way.

Assemble the tablecloth (B, a and b): First join three panels together as shown, along the A–B sides. Baste the side of one panel to overlap the side of another panel and zigzag the flat seam. Add the other section in the same manner. Baste and zigzag the rickrack braid along the two seams. Join the other panels together in the same way.

Join the two halves of the cloth across the centre. Baste and stitch them together as for the previous seams. Baste and zigzag stitch the braid right across the centre, covering all edges of seam and braid ends. Turn under a narrow hem all round the edge of the tablecloth and slip stitch, by hand or machine. Turn to the wrong side and trim off any ends close to the seams. Iron the tablecloth to finish.

Further suggestions: Try a smaller, more delicate cloth and embroider the seams, or reduce the pattern to make a round silk cushion (pillow). Instead of rickrack, trim with tartan ribbon or iron-on bias tape.

GARDEN CUSHION (PILLOW)
By Anne Hulbert

Hand-dyed, self-patterned and marbled cottons were used to make this eccentric log cabin cushion. There are 16 blocks, each having nine pieces. Each block has strong yellows and oranges as its main colour, with greens and blues alternating with hot reds and pinks. A plan for one block is given (A) which may be enlarged as required. The piecing is machined, using the 'stitch-and-flip' method. The cushion is filled with a light and bouncy polyester filling. It is trimmed with 'jumbo' piping and 16 'dolly' tassels made from the patchwork fabrics. The cushion measures approximately 60cm (24in) square, each block being 15cm (6in) square.

Materials
(quantities include seam allowances)

Cotton fabric for the cushion pad cover –
2 x 62.5cm (25in) squares
Filling for the pad – 1.5kg (50–60oz)
For templates – 25 x 30cm (10 x 12in) clear template plastic
Foundation – 64-cm (25-in) square of calico or firm cotton
Fabrics for patches, covering the jumbo piping cord and making the tassels – a total of approximately 3m (3¼ yd)

For the cushion back – a 64-cm (25-in) square of toning cotton
16 wooden or plastic beads, 15mm (⅝in) diameter
Jumbo piping cord – 2.8m (3yd)
Cotton yarn for attaching tassels to cushion – approximately 5.5m (6yd)
Matching threads

For the cushion pad: With right sides facing, stitch the two pieces together taking 12mm (½in) seam allowance and leaving a 30cm (12in) gap. Turn right side out. Insert the filling until the cushion is full, firm and free from lumps. Stitch across the gap.

To piece the front, trace off the nine pattern pieces on the plastic. Cut them out and mark the order of piecing as indicated on the plan. For one block, cut out an 18-cm (7-in) square of the foundation, slightly larger than the area of piecing. Mark round each template on the wrong side of the fabrics. These lines represent the stitching lines. Add the seam allowances by cutting out each piece 6mm (¼in) from the marked lines.

Baste patch 1, right side up, to the lower right-hand corner of the foundation as shown. With right sides facing, pin and stitch patch 2 to patch 1 onto the foundation as shown, B. Flip this back onto the foundation and iron the seam flat. Also with right sides facing, pin and stitch patch 3 to joined patches 1 and 2 as shown. Flip back and iron flat.

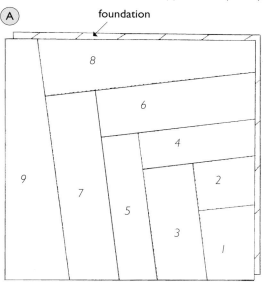

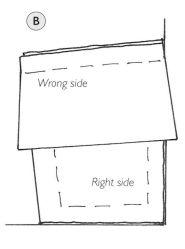

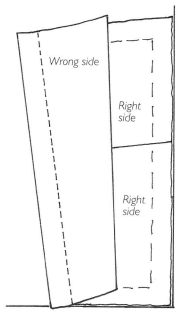

Block plan

Continue pinning, stitching, flipping and ironing patches in the same manner, in the order given, until the block is complete. Make the remaining blocks. Join the blocks together taking 6mm (¼in) seam allowances. Using the photograph as a guide, make four sets of four blocks with patch 1 of each block adjacent in the centre. Stitch the set of blocks together to complete the front.

Cut bias strips of fabric, 10cm (4in) wide, and totalling 2.72m (3yd) long to cover the jumbo cord (see Finishing Touches, for making the piping). Firmly baste the piping round the edge of the cushion front. Join the ends together at one side. Trim the cord ends to abut each other and neatly stitch them

together to secure. Fold one end of the fabric covering the cord under 6mm (¼in) and slip stitch it over the other end of the covered cord. Finish basting the piping to the cushion, then trim the cushion back to match the front.

With right sides facing, baste and stitch the front and back together, leaving a gap of 46cm (18in) at one side. Trim the edges and remove all basting stitches. Turn right side out. Insert the pad, ensuring that the corners fit well into the corners of the cover. Slip stitch across the gap.

Make 16 dolly tassels (see Finishing Touches). Stitch them to the piping to match up with the seams joining the blocks.

LUCY'S BOX
By Anne Hulbert

A collection of lively nursery prints was used to cover this child's seat/toy box, using the crazy strips method. The patches were cut in random rectangular pieces joined to make long strips. Iron-on bias tape covers and trims the joins of the long strips. The base and lid were lined with pieces of pretty wallpaper and trimmed with braid. Both were padded with cotton batting on the outside, before the patched covering was applied. Painted cupboard door knobs formed the feet and a small brass handle opens the box. The child's name was appliquéd on the top. Piecing and appliqué were machine stitched.

General materials required

A sturdy wooden box
Wallpaper (washable) and adhesive for lining
Staple gun and staples, or tacks and hammer
Sufficient braid, 2.5cm (1in) wide, to go around the inside of the lid and around the top edge inside the base, plus 15cm (6in) for turning the ends under
A small brass handle and 4 cupboard door knobs

Materials required for the crazy patchwork

First, measure the width, length and height of the box base and lid to estimate quantities of all the materials required – the cotton fabrics; firm iron-on fusible interfacing for the foundation; iron-on bias tape; cotton batting and a rotary cutter.

Note down the measurements and add about 10cm (4in) all round base and lid to allow for turnings, fitting and adjustments. Assemble plenty of printed cottons with complementary self-patterned cottons to use as plain colours, together with matching threads.

First, line the base and lid with the wallpaper. Cut out the two batting pieces to the measurements taken for the base and the lid.

To make the patchwork cover, see arrangement plan (A). Cut out the (fusible) foundation pieces to the measurements taken for

the base and lid. Cut out patches in random, more or less rectangular pieces, about 12cm (14¼in) wide, with lengths varying between 3.5 and 9cm (1½ and 3½in). With right sides facing, stitch them together to make enough long strips of sufficient length to cover the pieces of foundation. The photograph shows the direction of the long strips. Press all seams downwards.

A *Arrangement of patches*

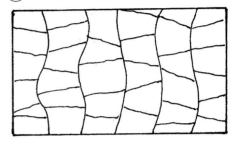

B *Cushion (pillow) using rich, plain shot silks and braid*

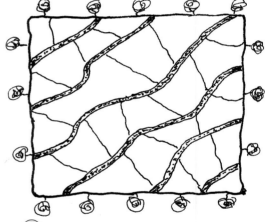

C *Roller blind (shade)*

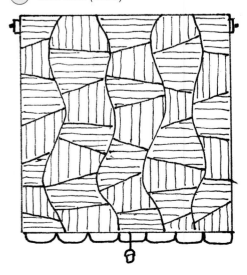

With right sides facing, lay these strips on top of each other in pairs – if manageable, several pairs at a time. Pin the pairs together to secure temporarily.

Using a rotary knife, cut the sides of the paired strips through the layers to produce wavy edges. Remove the pins.

Firmly iron the strips to the adhesive side of the foundation to bond well. Each strip should overlap the previous one by 3mm (⅛in). When the strips are well bonded, iron the bias tape over the overlapping edges to bond and cover them. Anchor the tape with zigzag stitching wide enough to penetrate each side of the tape. Set the stitch length to medium – 1½–2½.

If desired, cut out the child's name or initials in plain cotton. Use double-sided fusible fabric to bond the letters to the patchwork for the lid. Work close satin stitch to further secure. Staple, or tack, the batting pieces round the outside of the base and the top of the lid. Trim to just reach the edges. Fold the corners carefully to avoid unattractive lumps and trim off excess batting.

Staple, or tack, the completed crazy pieces to the base and lid. Pull the 'fabric' firmly (to eliminate wrinkles or slackness) over the batting onto the inside of the base and the lid to cover the wallpaper by about 18mm (¾in). Tack or staple to secure. Glue the braid round the inside of the base and lid to cover the stapled edges of fabric and wallpaper. Fix the handle in place and the 'knob' feet to the bottom of the box.

Further suggestions: Use similar crazy strip patchwork 'fabric' for making up into a screen, or a cushion (pillow) (B) or blind (shade) (C).

VICTORIAN STOOL COVER
By Anne Hulbert

With a Victorian stool in need of re-covering, what could be more appropriate than to make a piece of 'Victorian' crazy patchwork for it? The upholstery fabrics include a collection of rich colours and textures – chenilles, velvets, plushes, needlecords and corded silks. Random-cut patches overlap each other. Edges of patches are not turned under – fabric adhesive is used to apply them and also to check fraying. Machine satin stitch covers the seams and stitches the patches to a firm calico foundation. Two different colours are used: a bright cerise and a soft red, threaded together. The covered stool is finished with a double line of thick toning cord and corner rosettes made from crazy strips of toning silks.

Materials

Calico for the foundation
Plenty of patching fabrics
Fabric adhesive
Rayon thread for satin stitching
Polyester thread for the bobbin
A 'jeans' needle for stitching patches
For finishing: sufficient toning cord to reach twice round the stool, plus extra for joining 4 corner rosettes (see Finishing Touches)

Measure the stool (A). Add an extra 5–6cm (2–2½in) all round to provide generous allowances and cut out in the calico (B).

Divide the fabrics into groups according to colour and texture and experiment by laying them on the foundation to form an idea of what the finished piece might look like. Roughly cut out the first patch, four-sided with two sides to fit a corner. Spread a thin line of adhesive along the corner edges. Place the patch in a corner of the foundation to overlap the 'allowance' line by 6mm (¼in) as shown.

Roughly cut out a second patch. Apply a thin line of adhesive to each of the overlapping edges as before. Place it to overlap the first patch where necessary by 6mm (¼in) and also, where applicable, the 'allowance' line on the foundation, by 6mm (¼in).

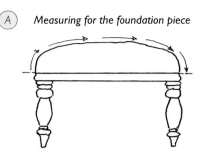

A *Measuring for the foundation piece*

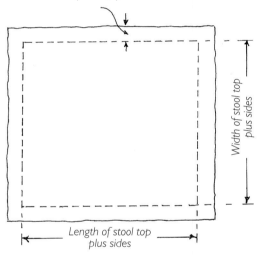

B *Foundation piece*

5–6cm (2–2½in) allowance all around

Width of stool top plus sides

Length of stool top plus sides

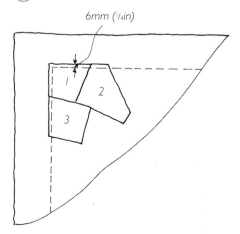

C *Applying the first patches*

6mm (¼in)

Continue adding patches, roughly cutting them out to overlap the previous ones, and always applying a thin line of adhesive to the overlapping edges. Subsequent patches can be cut to almost any shape that fits the spaces. When using the same fabric more than once, try changing the direction of the pile or grain. When seven or eight patches have been applied and the adhesive is completely dry, stitch them in place.

Thread a 'jeans' needle with both rayon threads together. Fill the bobbin with polyester thread. Set the stitch width to the widest and the stitch length as near zero as the machine can satin stitch comfortably. Work trial runs on the actual fabrics to be used, adjusting the settings as necessary. Continue the crazy patching until the area for the stool top is covered (see D). The newly created piece of crazy fabric is now ready to cover the stool.

Trim any excess fabric away from the edges and tack or staple to the stool, pulling the fabric firmly to avoid any wrinkles or slackness. Trim the fabric again, if necessary, to tidy the edges.

Spread a thin line of adhesive about 4cm (10in) along one end of the cord and press it firmly against the raw edge of the cover on one side of the stool. Pin the cord to hold it while the adhesive dries. Continue attaching the cord, a few inches at a time, twice round the stool. When the starting point is reached, trim the end and slide it under the starting end. Pull it through to conceal it.

To make the 10cm (4in) diameter rosettes, see Finishing Touches. The centres are small rosettes with a blob of stuffing inserted. They are then reversed, and stuck and stitched to the centres of the large rosettes. The complete rosettes are attached to the corners of the stool with a little adhesive and further secured with a few stitches at the back.

(D) *Patching completed*

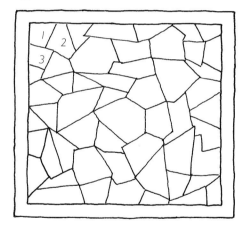

Chapter Fifteen
GALLERY

Thunderbird by Delia Salter

Inspiration for this quilt came from ancient rock carvings in Ontario. The quilt, which measures 147cm (58in) square, uses crazy patchwork extensively. Included in the quilt are hand-dyed and commercial silks and satins, pleats, tucks, fringed edges, photo transfers telling about Thunderbird in native legend, and hand and machine embroidery. Crazy-patched border motifs are appliquéd and the 'floating' feathers are two layers of fabric fused together. The piece is hand-quilted.

North Africa by Greta Fitchett

Made from brightly coloured cottons, the quilt, 112cm (44in) square, was inspired by fishing boats in Tunisia. The central panel is made by using fusible webbing to bond the appliqué pieces, which are further secured with free machine embroidery. White borders set off the hot colours. One of the border blocks is made from freely cut wavy lines appliquéd by machine. The piece is hand-quilted.

Pieces of the Sky by Delia Salter

One of a series of four small hangings based on the 'Elements', this one represents Air. The crazy-cut pieces include dyed and painted fabrics, some folded, some pleated and some with frayed raw edges. The piece, measuring 94 x 97cm (37 x 38in), is hand-quilted and embroidered with metallic thread.

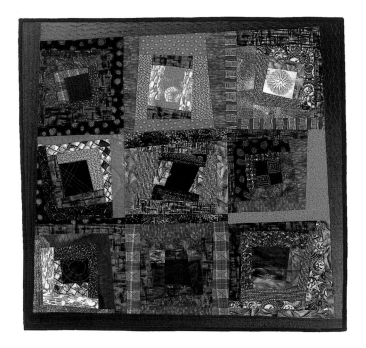

Bishop's Mitre by Nicola Bonner (top left)

The crazy log cabin hanging, 76cm (30in) square, is made from random-cut strips of printed cottons in the rich, dark ecclesiastical colours found in stained glass windows. The hanging is heavily quilted, following the pattern lines of the prints.

Signs of Spring by Celia Horsburgh (top right)

Small quilt, for hanging on a wall measuring 60cm (24in) square, features nine blocks of crazy log cabin in bright leaf greens surrounded by a border of greys. The yellow and green prairie points sewn into the blocks represent the first shoots of spring pushing through the ground.

Free Hand by Delia Salter (right)

The hanging, 60cm (24in) square, was made in a combination of dark red and lime-green hand-dyed and commercial fabrics. Crazy patchwork hands were appliquéd to crazy patchwork backgrounds. Further decoration includes embroidery, appliqué, beading, knotting and painted rickrack. The piece was hand-quilted with various colours and thicknesses of threads.

Baby's Play Mat
by Dorothy Stapleton

A detail of a crazy patchwork play mat for a young baby shows randomly cut patches, stitched by hand and machined to a foundation. The mat, measuring 91 x 137cm (36 x 54in), is made from printed panels and a variety of brightly coloured nursery fabrics.

Fire Screen
by Mary Lockie

In this work, measuring 66 x 86cm (26 x 34in), crazy patchwork makes a splendid backing for floral appliqué (broderie perse). The freely-cut patches were taken from a wide variety of green plain, printed and textured furnishing cottons. Fancy machine stitches decorate the seams. The work was enclosed in a glazed wooden frame with brass fittings.

132

Majestic by Karen Vickers

Nine crazy patchwork blocks, each with a four-sided starting patch, were made from vibrant silks and glitzy metallic fabrics. The green border of the hanging, which measures approximately 60cm (24in) square, is edged with appliquéd crazy triangles. These, in turn, are overlaid with larger sheer triangles with frayed edges.

Signs of Spring by Nicola Bonner

Crazy patchwork forms the basis of this textile picture, 60cm (24in) square, inspired by the New Forest in England. It makes an interesting backdrop for the trees, bluebells and paths. The trees were freely cut and applied. The flowers, ground cover and paths were machine-embroidered to complete the picture. Pale leaves were randomly cut from various green cottons and loosely stitched to the trees.

Evening bag by Jacqui Wood

The heavy silk bag features multi-coloured inserts of hand-dyed soft habutai silks. Randomly cut crazy strips are pieced onto a foundation using the stitch-and-flip method. The handle consists of a variety of matching yarns worked into a 3-ply plait.

Housewives' Lot
by Dorothy Stapleton

A detail of a humorous crazy patchwork quilt, which is made from a wide assortment of fabrics, including dishcloths. Patches were stitched to a foundation by hand and machine, and were then decorated with hand and machine embroidery. The piece, which measures 91 x 152cm (36 x 60in), is embellished with free-standing flowers, appliqué and quilting.

Joining Forces 4 – Tarantaal by June Barnes and Leslie Morgan

This is the fourth in a series of quilts made using the 'Stitching to Dye, Dyeing to Stitch' techniques developed by June Barnes and Leslie Morgan. Measuring 84 x 97cm (33 x 38in), the quilt was constructed by June Barnes using a random, crazy method of piecing. Black and white prints, viscose, velvet, satin and silk were used. When completed, the quilt was dyed orange. Leslie Morgan added dye paint to enhance the African impression.

Sunlight Through Stained Glass by Nicola Bonner (top left)

Inspired by the log cabin technique, this hanging, 71cm (28in) square, is formed from strips that are stitched to a foundation, starting with a randomly cut four-sided patch set at an angle. Each strip is freely cut to fit its space as required. Strips are sewn in turn to spiral round previous strips, using the stitch-and-flip method. The strips are cut wider and longer as work progresses.

Indian panel – maker unknown (top right)

An exotic Indian patchwork panel, 58cm (23in) square, is formed from crazy strips of magnificent heavy silk, silver and gold metallic, velvet and cotton fabrics. Thick black strips of fabric are couched along the seams. The pieces are extensively machine-embroidered in every shade of metallic threads. Several motifs are also richly embroidered in satin stitch in brown and black silk threads. The panel is very heavy.

Blossom by Blossom The Spring Begins by Frieda Oxenham (left)

Made with hand-dyed cottons, decorated with buttonhole stitch flowers and beads in the centre, this hanging measures 60cm (24in) square. The blocks are joined with beaded buttonhole stitches. Small transparent squares with frayed edges are applied to several areas prior to quilting.

Rocks at Coryton's Cove by Delia Salter

The colours in this wallhanging, 91cm (36in) square, depict the pink cliffs at Dawlish in Devon, England. Crazy patchwork techniques are combined with some freely cut strip piecing. The centre is embroidered with couched threads. The work is machine-quilted.

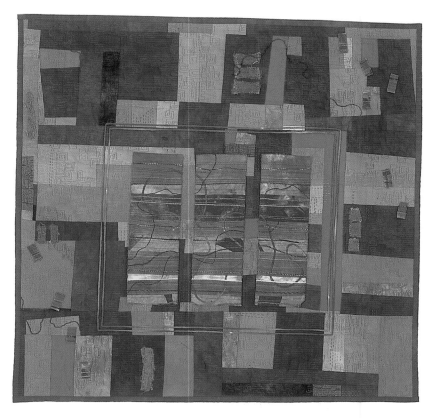

Some are Born to Sweet Delight by Frieda Oxenham

This quilt, 109cm (43in) square, uses silk, cotton, velvet and synthetic fabrics in delightfully refreshing oranges, yellows, pinks and creams. A black background sets off the colours perfectly. Nine blocks are worked in crazy log cabin patchwork. The quilt is decorated with interlaced buttonhole stitch, herringbone and running stitches. It is further embellished with a large variety of beads and sequins, which are also used to 'tie' the quilt layers together.

The Alchemist's Journey by Alicia Merrett (top left)

The cottons of this piece, which measures 112cm (44in) square, are all hand-dyed cotton fabrics, including the dark navy background. Freeform crazy cut patches were machine-pieced and the work was machine-quilted with metallic threads.

Flight of the Humming Bird by Alicia Merrett (top right)

Inspired by the vibrating wings and iridescent colours of the humming birds in Argentina, this piece, measuring 107 x 109cm (42 x 43in), was made with hand-dyed cottons and commercial black fabric background. Freeform, randomly cut patches were pieced by machine and the work was machine-quilted with metallic threads.

Colours Underfoot by Alicia Merrett (left)

This crazy log cabin, with some small pieces fused, is based on the actual colours found on the ground outside the maker's front door. The work, 60cm (24in) square, is made with hand-dyed cottons, cut freeform, and then pieced by machine. There is some fused appliqué and the patchwork was machine-quilted with rayon threads.

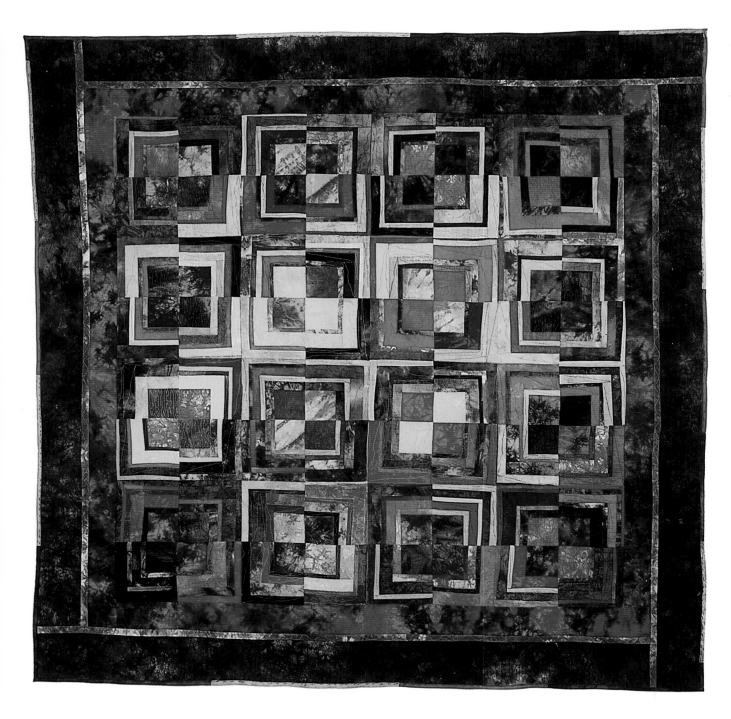

Keep Jammin' by Sandra Wyman

*Crazy log cabin and carnival colours inspired this
quilt, which measures approximately 152 x 182cm
(60 x 72in). The fabrics were hand-dyed, and the
patchwork was quilted both by hand and by free
machine stitching. It also includes 'in the ditch'
quilting along the seam lines.*

Seascape for Sergie
by Joy Real

The quilt, measuring approximately 122 x 182cm (48 x 72in), was made from recycled striped cotton shirting cut into crazy strips and stitched together to form varied shapes and sizes of blocks. Blocks were joined together to create a 'seaside' background for appliquéd seagulls, sail boats and fish. The quilt was one of 36 made by the Haslemere Embroiderers' Guild for the Chernobyl Children's Life Line.

MAIL ORDER SUPPLIERS

UNITED KINGDOM

Barnyarns Ltd Full range of Madeira threads for hand and machine embroidery; also fabrics, paints and needlework equipment; catalogue;
Tel. 01845 524344

Bits and Pieces Soft plain, patterned and metallic leathers and suedes; samples and catalogue –
4 Thorold Road, Bitterne Park, Southampton SO18 1JB; Tel. 01703 553334/266991

Charisma Beadwork Supplies C/o Phoenix Crafts, Dept. S, 25 Churchyard, Hitchen, Herts. SG5 1HP;
Tel. 01462 454 054

Craftswoman Fabrics 1st Floor, Unit 1, Kilroot Business Park, Carrickfergus, Co. Antrim BT38 7PR;
Tel. 02893 351277

Euro Japan Links Ltd Imported Japanese silks and cottons, plains and prints; embroidery fabrics and kits; catalogue and samples – 32 Nant Road, Child's Hill, London NW2 2AT;
Tel. 020 8201 9324

The Fabric Shop Patchwork and quilting fabrics, books and accessories; High Street,
Melrose TD6 9PA; Tel. 01896 823475

John Lewis and Co. Ltd Voiles, silks, cottons, braids and trimmings, paper patterns and haberdashery; branches in major cities

Mulberry Silks Hand-dyed embroidery threads, silk organza and ribbons – 2 Old Rectory Cottage, Easton Grey, Malmesbury, Wiltshire SN16 0PE;
Tel. 01666 840881

Oliver Twists Hand-dyed threads, fabrics and fibres – 34 Holmlands Park, Chester-le-Street, Co. Durham DH3 3JP; Tel. 0191 3888233

Patchwork Plus Everything for the needleworker – threads, fabrics, notions, charms and books – 129 Station Road, Cark, Grange-over-Sands, Cumbria. LA11 7NY; Tel. 015395 59009

Pearsall's Exclusive 'Filoselle' embroidery silk – Tancred Street, Taunton, Somerset TA1 1RY;
Tel. 01823 274700

Piecemakers: Plain and printed fleece by Anne Walker, 13 Manor Green Road, Epsom, Surrey. KT19 8RA; Tel. 01372 743161

The Quilt Room Everything necessary for patchwork, quilting and needlework; Rear Carvilles, Station Road, Dorking RH4 1XH; Tel. 01306 877307

Sew-Quick Sewing accessories, notions and a large range of needlework items and books –
17 Calside, Paisley, Renfrewshire, Scotland PA2 6DA; Tel. 0141 889 7333

The Silk Route Fine selection of silk threads and fabrics – a wide range from delicate chiffons to rich and textured silks – Hilary Williams, 32 Wolseley Road, Godalming, Surrey GU7 3EA;
Tel. 01483 420544

Stef Francis Space-dyed threads and fabrics. Large range of fabric types and textures and foils. Experimental packs. Waverley (ST), Higher Rocombe, Stoke in Teignhead, Newton Abbot, Devon, TQ12 4QL; Tel. 01803 823475

Variegations Unusual fabrics, threads, papers, metals, foils, beads and experimental packs – Rose Cottage, Harper Royd Lane, Norland, Halifax HX6 3QQ;
Tel. 01442 832411

Wendy Cushing Trimmings Ltd Braids, cords, rickrack braid, tassels and a wide range of trimmings – G7 Chelsea Harbour Design Centre, London SW10 0XE; Tel. 020 8556 3555

Whaley's Bradford Ltd Fabrics – Harris Court Road, Great Horton, Bradford, West Yorkshire BD7 4EQ;
Tel. 01274 576718

USA

Access Commodities Inc Suppliers of Au Ver a Soie silk embroidery threads – PO Box 1355, 1129 South Virginia Street, Terrell, Texas 75160;
Tel. (792) 563 3313

Bernina of America Sewing machines and sergers – 534 West Chestnut, Hinsdale, IL 60521 (Anne Hulbert uses and recommends Bernina machines)

The Cotton Patch A quilting supply store stocking over 700 solid cotton fabrics – 1025 Brown Avenue, Lafayette, CA 94549

Eagle Feather Trading Post Beads, buttons and doodads – 168 West 12th Street, Ogden, UT 84404

The Freed Company Beads and unusual findings – 415 Central N.W., Box 394, Albuquerque, NM 87103

Judith Designs Embellishments and findings for crazy patchwork, fabric kits, silk threads and ribbons – PO Box 177, Castle Rock, CO 80104

Kasuri Dyeworks Japanese fabrics, threads, books and dyes – 1959 Shattuck Avenue, Berkley, CA 94704

Kreinik Metallic Threads and Braids Soie Perlee, Soie Gobelins, Soie D'Alger Threads and Fine Cotton Threads; – Kreinik Customer Service Dept., Kreinik Manufacturing Co. Inc., Timanus Lane, Suite 101, Baltimore, MD 21244; Tel. (800) 537-2166

PFAFF American Sales Corp Sewing Machines – 610 Winters Avenue, Paramus, NJ 07653

Piecemakers 17–20 Adams Avenue, Costa Mesa, California 92626. Suppliers for crazy patchwork, quilting, embroidery, beadwork and ribbonwork.

Rupert Gibbon and Spider Inc. Jacquard fabric paints – PO Box 425, Healdsburgh, CA 95448

SCS USA Madeira Embroidery and Decorative Sewing Threads – 9631 NE Colefax Street, Portland, OR 97220-1232; Tel. (503) 252-1452

Timber Lane Press Tintex Interfacing – North 22700 Rim Rock, Hayden Lake, Idaho 83835
Treadleart Embroidery Supplies, Books, Fabrics and Sewing Accessories – 25834 Narbonne Avenue, Lomita, CA 90717
YLI Embroidery – PO Box 109, Provo, UT 84601

AUSTRALIA
Anne's Glory Box Quilting, Needlework and Embroidery Supplies, plus Laces and Books – 60–62 Beaumont Street, Hamilton, New South Wales 2303
The Thread Studio Art and Embroidery Supplies – 6 Smith Street, Perth WA 6000

NEW ZEALAND
Craft Suppliers 31 Gurney Road, Belmont, Lower Hutt, New Zealand
Margaret Barnet Distributors Ltd Needle-arts supplies – 19 Beasley Avenue, PO Box 12-034, Penrose, Auckland, NZ 64-9-525-6142

FURTHER READING

UNITED KINGDOM
Beverley, Deena *Ribboncraft,* London, Mitchell Beazley, 1997
Campbell-Harding, Valerie *Fabric Printing for Embroidery*, London, B.T. Batsford, 1990
Campbell-Harding, Valerie and Watts, Pamella *Bead Embroidery*, London, B.T. Batsford, 1993
Colby, Avril *Patchwork*, London, B.T .Batsford, 1958
Eaton, Jan *The Mary Thomas Dictionary of Embroidery Stitches*, revised colour edition of the 1934 original, London, Brockhampton Press, 1988
Holmes, Val *The Machine Embroiderers' Workbook*, London, B.T. Batsford, 1991
Hulbert, Anne *Creative Beadwork*, London, Bartholomew, 1976;
Hulbert, Anne *Folk Art Quilts* London, Collins and Brown, 1992;
Hulbert, Anne *Machine Quilting and Padded Work* London, B.T. Batsford, 1991
Kirby, H and C. *Floral Transfers*, Tunbridge Wells, UK, Search Press, 2000
Montano, Judith, Baker *Elegant Stitches*, Lafayette, CA, C and T Publishing, 1995
Tucker, Dorothy *Appliqué*, London, B.T. Batsford, 1989

*Note: If books marked * are not available, they can be borrowed from any of the Public Lending Libraries.*

US PUBLISHERS OF RELEVANT BOOKS
American School of Needlework Consumer Division, 1455 Linda Vista Drive, San Marcus, CA 92069
C and T Publishing PO Box 1456, Lafayette, CA 94549
Dover Publications Inc. 31 East 2nd Street, Minneola, NY 11501-3582
Krause Publications 700 East State Street, Iola, WL 54990-0001; Tel. (800) 258 0929
The Quilt Digest Press/NTC Contemporary Publishing Group Inc. 4255 West Touhy Avenue, Lincolnwood (Chicago), Illinois, 60646-1975

ORGANIZATIONS AND MAGAZINES

UNITED KINGDOM
The Embroiderer's Guild Apartment 41, Hampton Court Palace, Surrey KT8 9AU; Tel. 020 8943 1229
Fabrications with Patchwork, Quilting & Embroidery magazine, published by Grosvenor Publishing 21 High Street, Spalding, Lincs. PE11 1TX; Tel. 01775 712100
Popular Patchwork magazine, published by Nexus Special Interests Nexus House, Azalea Drive, Swanley, Kent BR8 8HU; Tel. 01322 660070/722900
The Quilter's Guild of Great Britain, Room 190, Dean Clough, Halifax, West Yorkshire HX3 5AX
The Quilter magazine, published by The Quilter's Guild of Great Britain (see above)
The Royal School of Needlework Apartment 12a, Hampton Court Palace, KT8 9AU; Tel. 020 8943 1432
Stitch with the Embroiderer's Guild magazine (see above)
The World of Embroidery magazine, published by The Embroiderer's Guild (see above)

USA
The American/International Quilt Association PO Box 19126, Houston, Texas TX 79126; Tel. (713) 978 7054
The Embroiderer's Guild of America Inc. 335 West Broadway, Suite 100, Louisville, KY 40202; Tel. (502) 689-6956
The National Quilting Association PO Box 393, Elliot City, MD 21043-0393; Tel. (301) 461-5733
Piecework Magazine Interweave Press 201 East Fourth Street, Loveland, CO 80537-5655
Quilter's Newsletter Magazine Leman Publication Inc., 6700 W. 47th Ave, PO Box 394, Wheatridge, CO 80034-0394

MUSEUMS

UNITED KINGDOM

The American Museum in Britain Claverton Manor, Bath, Avon BA2 7BD; Tel. 01225 460503
The Beamish North of England Open Air Museum Beamish Hull, Stanley, County Durham DH9 0RG; Tel. 01207 231811
The Royal Albert Memorial Museum Queen Street, Exeter, Devon EX4 3RX
The Victoria and Albert Museum Cromwell Road, South Kensington, London SW7 2RL; Tel. 020 7938 8441
Worthing Museum and Art Gallery Chapel Road, Worthing, East Sussex BN11 1HD; Tel. 01903 239999

US

Note: America is a vast country and almost every state has museums in which examples of crazy patchwork may be found.

Illionois State Museum Cnr. Spring and Edwards Streets, Springfield, IL 62706; Tel. 217 782 7836
The Kansas City Museum of History and Science Crazy and Log Cabin quilts – 3218 Gladstone Boulevard, Kansas City, MO 64123
The Museum of American Folk Art Antique quilts – 444 Park Ave South, New York City, NY 10016; Tel. (212) 481 3080
The Oakland Museum Crazy quilts – 1000 Oak Street, Oakland, CA 94607; Tel. (415) 273 3402
The Shelburne Museum US Rt. 7, Shelburne, VT 05482; Tel. (802) 985-3346

ACKNOWLEDGEMENTS

MANUFACTURERS

The author would like to thank the following companies for their kind contribution of materials and helpful advice:
Coats Crafts UK – for permission to reproduce the embroidery diagrams from their leaflets; telephone Helpline 01325 365457 for details of availability and stockists
Craftswoman Fabrics – for supplying specialized fabrics – metallics, velvets, glitz and fleece; write to 1st. Floor, Unit 1, Kilroot Business Park, Carrickfergus, Co. Antrim, N. Ireland BT38 7PR
Dylon International Ltd – for their help, advice and information; send SAE to Consumer Advice, Lower Sydenham, London SE26 5HD, or call 020 8663 4296 for information
Gutterman Threads – for supplying multicoloured polyester and machine embroidery threads; enquiries to Perivale-Guttermann Ltd, Wadsworth Road, Greenford, Middlesex UB6 7JS
Madeira Threads UK – for supplying metallic and rayon threads; for information and stockists write to Thirsk Industrial Park, York Road, Thirsk, N. Yorks YO7 3BX
Rowan Textiles – for supplying a selection from Kaffe Fassett's patchwork fabric collection; telephone 01484 681881 for local and mail order stockists
Vilene Retail UK – for supplying examples of fusible bonding fabrics; enquiries and catalogue, P.O. Box 3, Greetland, Halifax, West Yorks HX4 8NJ
Vita Fibres – for supplying a wide variety of batting fabrics; enquiries to Lower lane, Milnrow, Rochdale OL16 4NP

GUILDS

Acknowledgements are due to the members of The Berwick-upon-Tweed branches of the Embroiderers' Guild and the Quilters' Guild, with a very special thank you to Jill Curry, Sheena Henderson, Audrey Kenny, Mary Lockie, Frieda Oxenham, Sarah Mitchell and Hazel Shell for their kind help and support.
The Quilters' Guild of The British Isles very kindly lent photographs of antique works from their Heritage Collection – arranged by Celia Eddy.

JOURNALS

The author is most grateful to the editors of the following publications for introducing her to the makers of some of the work exhibited in the Gallery: *Fabrications*, *Popular Patchwork*, *The Quilter* (the journal of The Quilters' Guild of The British Isles), and *Stitch*.

CRAFTSWOMEN

The author is very grateful indeed to everybody who kindly lent their lovely work for the text and the projects, and especially to those who contributed to the superb collection of work featured in the Gallery. Their inspirational projects have clearly contributed to the revival of this aspect of patchwork.

INDEX